Confessions
of a Food Catholic

Published by Canon Press
P.O. Box 8729, Moscow, Idaho 83843
800.488.2034 | www.canonpress.com

Interior design by Valerie Anne Bost.
Cover design by James Engerbretson.

Printed in the United States of America.

Unless otherwise noted, all Bible quotations are from the King James Version.

Library of Congress Cataloging-in-Publication Data:
Names: Wilson, Douglas, 1953- author.
Title: Confessions of a food Catholic / Douglas Wilson.
Description: Moscow : Canon Press, 2016.
Identifiers: LCCN 2016026903 | ISBN 9781944503475 (pbk.)
Subjects: LCSH: Food--Religious aspects--Christianity. | Dinners and
      dining--Religious aspects--Christianity.
Classification: LCC BR115.N87 W565 2016 | DDC 261.5/6--dc23
LC record available at https://lccn.loc.gov/2016026903

16 17 18 19 20 21 22   9 8 7 6 5 4 3 2 1

Confessions
of a Food Catholic

DOUGLAS WILSON

canonpress
Moscow, Idaho

*This book is dedicated to all those at church dinners
who I noticed didn't have enough protein on their plates
and who tried to cover it up by noticing
I didn't have enough greens on mine.*

Contents

You Talkin' to *Me?*

Many years ago, when I was in a band, I came home one evening after a practice or a gig or something. I say this because I remember this incident vividly, and I was carrying my guitar. The kids were in bed, and my wife, Nancy, met me at the door very worried about something. Our duplex apartment was full of a foul smell—and it was really bad. Nancy has an acute sense of smell, and she often smells things that I don't, but this odor registered with both of us in a big way. She was worried about a possible chemical leak in the neighborhood—something like that—and the question was whether we needed to get the kids up and out of there. Before we did that, I began hunting around outside our apartment, looking for some dead critter in the junipers right below the windows. In the course of this investigation, I stumbled across the problem. Our Korean neighbors were having a social get-together, and they were cooking up a batch of ethnic food with their friends, just like mama used to make.

Now it takes all kinds, and I can't tell you how much this story has delighted me over the years. But I have not just been delighted because *I* thought it was foul, but it also delighted me that our triune God made people's tastes so different. It delights me that *they* thought it was wonderful. I thought it was foul, but I probably need to get out more. This story should set the stage for what follows in this book.

My purpose in writing on this subject is that I have seen a number of Christians developing an extremely unscriptural approach to food. And by this, I do not mean that they have started to like things I don't like, or have started to dislike things I like very much. The issue is not one of taste. This is a free country. Make your own choices. You should be able to go to Arby's *or* Wendy's. *Joke.* Seriously, joke. Difference in taste is one of the things that keeps us from becoming boring, and keeps us reflecting the infinite character and nature of God. So hooray for differences in taste, whether individual or cultural.

Neither am I a "food egalitarian." There is great cooking, good cooking, so-so cooking, poor cooking, and carrots out of the bag. Men and women exercise dominion in this area, just as we do in others, and this means that there will be a varied range of accomplishments, with some of them being more praiseworthy than others. So I am not saying that there are no qualitative differences between foods.

Neither is it my intent to say that the apostle Paul, when he said that the weaker brother eats only vegetables, was talking directly about our modern forms of vegetarianism. Of course not. But what he said *applies* to modern vegetarianism. The same thing goes for the ritual defilements from food that the Jews were so concerned about. A rabbi's religious loathing of bacon proceeded from a very different source than does a modern (quasi-religious) loathing of refined sugar. The difference is that the rabbi at least had *some* passages to back him up. My argument here is *a fortiori*—if Jesus declared all ritually unclean foods from the Old Testament clean (representing the Gentiles as they did), then how much more are *all* foods declared clean? If *bacon* is now clean, then how could it be possible for processed cheese *not* to be? And if processed cheese had somehow become unclean, wouldn't God have told us about it?

My point is *not* that sinning with food is impossible. A man can sin by not sharing it, by eating way too much of it, by throwing it across the cafeteria, and so forth. My point is that a man *cannot* sin by bowing his head over it, saying grace with true gratitude in his heart, and then tucking in—and this truth is not affected by whether what he is about to eat is a chocolate pudding cup from a fast food joint or lots of spinach, rich in iron.

So the comparatively new and alarming trend in Christian circles toward the demonization of certain basic foods is the sin I particularly want to address.

I am *not* speaking of those who have genuine allergies, but rather to a larger, culture-wide despising of things that God gave to us, having first pronounced them good. I am speaking (to take just two examples) of whole milk straight out of cows, and gluten straight out of a wheat field. To make my point clearer—yay, fat! yay, gluten!

Someone with a genuine allergy takes it as a hard providence that he cannot drink milk anymore. He really is lactose intolerant, and it tears him up every time he thinks of how much he used to enjoy a mounded bowl of cookies and cream. But when someone else reacts to milk in an *ick, poo!* fashion, the problem is something else altogether. For many people in this latter category, the language of allergies, or faux-medicine from some guru, or "Bible diets," can provide useful temporary cover, at least until more Christians can be persuaded to join them in their gnostic orcification of the good stuff.

And don't write me an earnest letter claiming that all the "good stuff" was inserted by our evil factories. The devil isn't that generous. Food phobias have a long and rooted history in American Christianity, and they are in the middle of a strong comeback. Neither should anyone write me a letter claiming that I have said there is no such thing as a genuine food allergy. There certainly is, just as there are people in the world with a missing leg. My point, and I am seeking to make it carefully here, is that people with two legs are not restricted to one leg, and that it is better to have two. And it is not to the point to say that I am making light of the tragedy of having just one leg. No, I am actually trying to point out another tragedy of two-legged people hopping around unnecessarily—all because they read a book that seemed quite persuasive.

I am not going to make my case for it here, but simply state the conclusion, let that settle in, and try to argue for it later: A large part of the reason that Christians are pulling away from certain foods with loathing is the result of father hunger. When you learn the meaning of fatherhood, you have learned the goodness of *provision*.

These qualifications should make it clear that I am not mocking the sick and the infirm, or being hard-hearted toward those who are truly hurting. Nor are these qualifications simply a *pro forma* sort of thing, giving myself plausible deniability, in case someone's feelings get hurt and I wanted to have something to point to while maintaining that I didn't *say* that. I really believe my qualifications.

Here is another full paragraph of them, and a longish paragraph it is too. First, I understand that these things operate on a sliding scale—it is not the case that you either go to the hospital all swoll up with your life on the line, or your problem is entirely imaginary. Some allergies are very serious immediately, while others should be filed under certain foods "not agreeing with" your constitution. There are food allergies, with varying degrees of seriousness, and there are food intolerances, with varying degrees of seriousness. The law of love should govern in all instances. Hosts should be thoughtful hosts, and guests should be thoughtful guests. Also, when it comes to particular cases and instances, with people I deal with directly, I am not trigger-happy in offering the suggestion that the problem might not be "real." Actually, the problem is always real in some way, but it is sometimes not real in the way that everybody first thought. But if I am counseling someone, for example, and begin to suspect that some kind of self-delusion is going on, it will usually take me months to get to the point where I would suggest that directly. There would be a lot of other ground to cover first. And what this means is that I am not making snap-diagnoses at a distance of particular individuals in any of my writing on this subject.

I have been dealing with people in pastoral ministry for decades, and have pretty much seen it all. I have seen enough to know that there is a true category out there of hypochondria, and there is another category of people who are genuinely sick—and some of them with illnesses that are quite mysterious, and hard to pin down. Now the fact that I believe there is such a thing as the former category does not mean that I deny the existence of the second, or the seriousness of what people in the second category face, or the difficulties they confront when they are afflicted with something that might look to outsiders like they are making it all up. To all such—my heart goes out to them, and they don't have worry about any snide comments from me. I have never been talking about them.

This being the case, why do I run the risk of being misunderstood by some with a genuine ailment? When I am attacking abuse in this area (as I frequently do), it is because I have seen the real damage, in real time, that play-acting can do to marriages, families, and friendships. I have also seen a situation where someone in genuine pain just soldiers on through because she will not be lumped in with those who have their boutique allergies. This is a situation created by the fakery, and not by recognition that there is such a thing as fakery or self-deception.

Here are the principles I am most concerned about:

1. The first point is that table fellowship is one of the most important ecclesiastical issues found in the New Testament. We need to remember that, and act accordingly. Some of the fiascoes I have seen were the result of ignoring that truth. We have gotten to the point where there is widespread disruption of such table fellowship, and I simply think that more of us should act like it is a big deal. Just to be clear on the point, genuine food allergies, etc. do *not* disrupt table fellowship because they provide an occasion for love. The disruption is caused by manipulation and selfishness, which is the opposite of *koinonia* fellowship.

2. The second issue concerns the nature of knowledge. I could care less what other people eat—provided

they are having a good time with it. But I care very much about truth and verification. I care very much about irrationality being given a free pass simply because it is what Smith or Murphy "are into." Once the principles of unreason are well-established in our midst, we will find that we cannot turn them off with a switch, simply because we are now dealing with something more serious. We are to love the Lord our God with all our minds, and I have to say that I have seen some striking instances of that not happening. The *post hoc* fallacy is not the queen of the sciences.

3. The third point concerns frequent abdication on the part of fathers and husbands. Many times, emotional and spiritual issues show up in the lives of women as food issues, and the men involved are often too weak, or cowardly, or defensive about their own causal role, to address it in the way they ought to. Women are prone to be deceived (1 Tim. 2:14), and men are prone to let them be deceived. This is an area where I have seen radical unsubmissiveness on the part of some wives, and radical cowardice on the part of some husbands, conspiring together to destroy families. The food is just a symptom; the real problem is located somewhere else entirely. And wives, don't read this and go off to demand that your husband tell you if this is true in your case. It might not be, but if it

is, you are unlikely to get a straight answer from him. Get on your knees and ask the Spirit if it is true. *He's not afraid of you.*

4. And last, if any reacted to my earlier use of the phrase boutique allergies, and assume that anyone who uses phrases like that must be attacking you individually, then this illustrates the heart of the problem with "qualifications." There is no good reason I can think of for someone with a real broken leg being defensive on behalf of someone who is faking a broken leg. To make the point bluntly, referring back to my second concern, if I write that Smith is faking his broken leg, it is not germane to the discussion to point to a picture of your son, who is not a Smith at all, with the bone sticking out. My belief that there is such a thing as a boutique allergy industry does not mean that I believe that you are a customer. I mean, I don't even know your name. But those shops are out there, and they do have customers.

So if genuine sufferers are not my target audience, then who is? Let me put this one in the categories of two different prepositions—at and for. Who is this book aimed *at*, and who is it *for*?

It is directed at every species of phood pharisees. Some may think that such legalism mostly a windmill to tilt at, but I think differently. I see and hear expressions of moral superiority based on personal food choices on a regular basis, and such expressions are a true enemy of our souls. They are deadly.

This is quite a different thing than a recognition that some foods can be better than others—aesthetically, nutritionally, and so forth. Avoidance of pharisaism is not equivalent to food relativism—though the pharisees usually think that it is. If *their* made-up rules fall, then all moral standards must topple with them, and civilization with it. Or so they think.

What comes to mind when you imagine a person with a seared conscience? The first thing might be a sociopath—someone who has no compunction about doing anything whatever. "Speaking lies in hypocrisy; having their conscience seared with a hot iron . . ." (1 Tim. 4:2). That is a natural move, but it is a mistaken one. In scriptural terms, when a person's conscience is seared with a hot iron, he doesn't become an anarchist, he becomes a fierce moralist. Notice the next verse—"forbidding to marry, and commanding to abstain from meats, which God hath created to be received with thanksgiving of them which believe and know the truth" (1 Tim. 4:3). A man with a seared conscience is the prohibitionist, the wowser, the fusser.

On reflection, this should not be surprising. As long as we bear the image of God, we have to function in terms of antithesis, in the light of a foundational right and wrong. But because we are in rebellion against God, we violate His holy commandments. But we still have a need to *feel* righteous, and we have a desperate need to shout down our guilt. What better way to shout down the guilt than to go on a compensatory crusade? This is displaced moralism.

Thus we have a man who screams at his wife, but who drives a Prius with a smug look, a man who uses porn, but who is fastidious about avoiding gluten, a woman who has a botoxed face and siliconed chest, but who eats plenty of leafy greens because it seems "more natural," a man beset with homosexual lusts who is on a fierce crusade for wealth redistribution, and so on.

Nothing is being said here about the gourmand who knows and understands good food, and would consequently prefer a meal bursting with the interplay of numerous intelligently placed spices to a meal on the couch from a crinkly bag, the name of which ends with that pervasive food group suffix -itos. That is simply a man getting good at something, just like other men get good on the guitar, or laying down asphalt, or building skyscrapers, or writing novels. Good on him, and maybe he should think about becoming a chef.

No, I am talking about the crusader, the devotee. I am talking about the person who, having eaten the *cibus prohibitus*, feels guilty. I am talking about the person who, observing his brother at Quiznos (from a high and lofty perspective), feels censorious.

The point is not just that this displaced moralism is a bad thing in itself, which it is. The point is that it is often a smoke-screen distraction, an attempt to persuade himself, his family, his church, and his pastor, that he is a morally serious person—despite the hidden drunkenness, porn, anger, homosexuality, and so on. We are so constituted that we do not just set aside the Word of God. We do it *by means of* our own traditions.

So that is where this book is aimed. If you're not living in Phariseeville, then, as the Aussies say, no worries. If you have never seen an instance of phood pharisaism, and you don't know *what* I am talking about, then perhaps you should consider whether you are one. But if like the rest of us you do live in a society that is given over to this foolishness, then it would be difficult not to be affected by it all. But being affected by pharisees is not the same thing as being one, and those in that category can find themselves being pushed in a direction they haven't really thought about much.

So if you assume that natural, ancient, and organic *always* means healthier, then this book is for you. Something could genuinely be all three and still be bad for you. If you tend to think that natural on a label is anything other than an advertising hook, manipulated and controlled by bureaucrats and corporate execs, this book is for you. If you think that you (or your children) ought to be required to eat the heel of the loaf because the browner and tougher it is, the more nutritious it must be, then this book is for you.

Lastly, and above all, if you think that all these things are rules for *holiness,* and consequently that those who aren't following them aren't holy and therefore deserve your righteous condemnation, then this book is *most definitely* for you.

CHAPTER 1

Standards True and False

The position I am arguing for is not food egalitarianism or, worse, food relativism. There is no neutrality anywhere, including in the kitchen and dining room, and this means that in principle we can say that "this food" is better than "that food." But when we do, we are making an aesthetic and practical judgment grounded in a biblical worldview. We are making a judgment that has moral implications (as everything does)—but we are *not* making a moral judgment on individual behavior.

A moral judgment proper says that if you commit adultery, you have sinned. If you steal something from the local drugstore, you have sinned. An aesthetic judgment with moral implications is a very different thing. A practical judgment with moral implications is a very different thing.

But the legalistic mind is a simplistic mind and doesn't want to grapple with any of this stuff. In that mindset, if something has negative moral implications then we must have the authority to make a moral judgment on anyone participating in that thing at any level. But the Bible doesn't address broad moral situations in this fashion at all.

The biblical commandments tell us what the sins are. The biblical worldview tells us what the moral ramifications are. *But we are not allowed to generate new commandments from those ramifications*, even as we labor and pray for those ramifications.

Eating meat offered to idols provides one example. Christians remaining in the Roman army would be another. Christians serving as tax collectors for a pagan system would be another. Daniel serving as the chancellor of the University of Babylon is another. Scripture is full of believers participating in subpar systems—as weighed in the balances of a biblical worldview—and it does not follow from this that such participation was sinful. Since we are allowed to look to these instances as exemplars, the opposite follows. To participate enthusiastically in the midst of a sinful set-up (like the *world*) is not the same thing as sinning. To make such an illegitimate jump is to create the basis for suffocating legalisms.

In principle, all Christians would be immediately paralyzed, were they consistent with this approach, because virtually every transaction in this sinful world has the ramification, at some level, of keeping some unbeliever or unbelieving system going. To buy gas at a convenience store that sells porn keeps the porn industry going. To buy groceries from a grocery store owned by Mormons keeps their false doctrine going. To ride in a car built by non-Christians to go to the gas station or grocery store is to add a second layer to your perfidious conduct. And there are about a thousand layers to go. This is just like the house that Jack built.

Now in the past, I have inveighed (on aesthetic grounds, with moral implications) against Thomas Kinkade paintings, wearing gym shorts and flip flops to church, three-chord treacle songs, church architecture that looks like an attempt to be a mid-range mall, and the aesthetic howlers associated with every form of faux-authenticity (factory-torn jeans, paint spatters extra). Why wouldn't I be willing to do the same kind of thing with food? Oh, but I *am*. This is exactly the same kind of deal.

I believe that we as Christians are called to cultivate cultural maturity over time, and that in every

generation there will be people in the vanguard trying to show the way. They will be headed in the right
direction, and they will know that none of us have
arrived or attained, and that we will be centuries getting there. But they are confident, joyful, and glad
nonetheless. At the same time, there will be others
claiming to know the way, and they will have *strict*
and detailed instructions for the rest of us proles.
They are fussers and cranks, whose chief delight in
life is having something or someone to look down on.
The realm of food is a prime breeding ground for this
second kind of person, although they often pretend,
as necessary, to be the first kind of person.

So, if we are engaged in trying to raise the standard when it comes to what and how we eat, how do
we proceed? What do we need to remember?

First, everything is grounded in the nature and
character of God. We are Trinitarians, which means
that we must not look for our eating habits to be any
kind of monochrome affair. How will the new human
race that is being established in the world display
the infinite and astonishing character of this God?
Will it all end with everybody eating the same taste-
less oatmeal-like paste for every meal, no sugar, no
cream? No . . . wrong God. Aesthetic judgments that
are grounded in the character of God are tricky if we

have a false picture of this God. If we think that creation is a pyramid and God is the mathematical apex, then there is room for only one beautiful thing there, if that. This is a false move that gets us, at best a functional unitarianism, and at worst, mathematical point atheism. But Flannery O'Connor notwithstanding (with her *everything that rises must converge* stuff), when we get to the top, we find that it is infinite there. Further up and further in. The peak is bigger than the base of the mountain.

What this means is our attempts to reduce aesthetic judgments to the level of a footrace are misguided in the extreme. When we judge a footrace, what we need is a stopwatch. When we judge a painting, a dance, or a superb five-star meal, far more is going on. Some defend objective beauty (as they ought to), but they approach aesthetics simplistically, with a stopwatch. Others see how difficult it is, needing to involve much more than a stopwatch, and conclude that it must be impossible, and veer into an incoherent relativism.

Second, our pattern in this world is the life of the Church. We should worship every Lord's Day, with joy and exuberance, confessing our sins, hearing the Word, and sitting down every week in the heavenly places for a simple meal of bread and wine. We are to do so free from all guilt and shame, accepted by the Father. This is the bedrock upon which we are to build everything in our week, which means that we should be growing to the point where we take *all* our meals free of guilt and shame, and where saying grace with gratitude over everything we ingest is not an empty ritual. We are really thankful for it. We are on a pilgrimage, which means that we are not there yet. We must be *content* with not being there yet. We are helped on the way by the Lord's Spirit because we are not there yet. Insistence that we "attain" right now, in any area, is simply an ungodly impatience. But discontent and impatience set us back. If we pursue something because we really like it, we are growing in our understanding in the way we ought to, without fussing, and without guilt.

Twenty years ago, Nancy and I did not know nearly as much about wines as we do know. Were we in sin back then? What kind of question is that? We live in the Pacific Northwest, which has pioneered the ideal of the coffee aesthetic. Was that a good development? Sure, so long as it is driven by learning and appreciation and gladness, and not by snobbery. We should pursue the ideal of good cooking and good food the same way—free from guilt, free from snobbery, free from lies about cooties in the food.

Third, recognize that in this fallen world we are striving to mature in a number of different areas at the same time. This means a series of trade-offs. For a harried mother striving to be "reformational" in her approach to her domestic challenges, she might find herself (multiple times a day) having to choose between this and that, both options insisting that they represent a higher and better way. She can cook the kids a real meal, hot and nutritious, ready at six, or she can get the laundry done and have their sheets changed, clean and fresh, ready by bedtime. But not both. They can have the reformational meal, and deal with the sheets for one more night, or they can enjoy clean sheets after a dinner of pancakes. In this life, perfectionism is paralyzing. Strive for excellence while taking it easy.

Fourth, recognize that striving to improve in this way cannot be separated from the economic realities. Money is one of the factors in the trade-offs. If you choose to buy the best produce, for example, you are going to pay more for it. If you are paying top dollar for such things, then don't pretend you are doing something else. Recognize that you are comparatively rich, and that you are using your disposable income on luxuries. One of saddest features (or funniest, depending) of contemporary food snobbery is the notion that rich people are getting in touch with the rhythms of the earth when they shop at the Whole Foods market. Paying three times as much for a really good apple is a fine thing to do, so long as you know that you are doing it. But if you think that you are a humble creature of the soil because you are whooping it up on luxuries is one of the oddest things that I have ever seen in my life. I understand, to return to an earlier example, why people would come to the point where they would be willing to drop five bucks on a cup of coffee. Okay, I think. It's a free country and you obviously have a lot of money. And if you don't have a lot of money, or you haven't bought into the aesthetic coffee imperative, I understand staying with the older drip coffee. Great. Still a free country. But what I don't get is the idea of someone spending five dollars on a cup of coffee as a way of expressing solidarity with peasants the world over. Look, you're rich. Come to terms with it.

Fifth, striving for cultural maturation includes the recognition that context matters. When we use the expression "good clothes" we know that a wedding tuxedo fits in that category, and coveralls for changing the oil in the car do not. But this general tag should not mislead. The tuxedo is an *inferior* clothing choice if what you are doing is changing the oil in the car. Depending on context, the superior item is often the inferior choice. To use another illustration I have used before, a cathedral is a superior architectural specimen to a typical suburban house. But a suburban house is far superior if the task at land is frying up some bacon or watching Monday Night Football.

Food choices function the same way. The very best food possible is not the very best choice for every occasion. Distinguish between steak dinners for your anniversary and Cheerios in the morning.

We have set up many standards, true and false, by which we evaluate our food choices. I'll examine several of those in more detail over the course of the next few chapters.

CHAPTER 2

Nouvelle Kosher

F oodolatry is a besetting sin of ours. James
Jordan writes,

Fringe groups in American Christianity have
for almost two centuries advocated dietary and
hygienic practices designed to curb sin, and this
is part of the milieu in which the current discussion must take place. It seems reasonable to many
Americans to assume that God intended to teach
Israel about diet, because diet and health are part
of the popular civil religion of America today, and
because dietetic theology has been a strong current in American Christianity in the past. In the
nineteenth century there were prominent liberal
and sectarian theologians who believed that the
sinfulness of man could be curbed through diet

and hygiene. John Harvey Kellogg, a Seventh-Day Adventist, invented corn flakes as a meatless breakfast food designed to reduce the sexual drive. Control of 'bestial sexual impulses' was linked in the popular imagination, both sectarian and liberal, with a bland diet devoid of alcohol, coffee, tea, tobacco, condiments, and largely devoid of meat. Assumption of this diet would reduce what is today called libido, and this reduction of the 'animal' in man would be passed on to one's children, who would grow up with less 'original sin.' Salvation through diet passed into the popular imagination through the writings of liberals like Horace Bushnell, sectarians like Kellogg and Charles Finney, and cultists like Mary Baker Eddy. As a result there is a pervasive orientation toward dietetic theology in American Christianity that colors our discussion of the Sinaitic dietary laws.[1]

And from a footnote on the same pages, less original sin "was the purpose of Graham flour, developed by Sylvester Graham, and still with us in Graham Crackers. The Graham diet was used at Charles Finney's Oberlin College to protect students against 'vile affections.' The Bill Gothard Institute is strongly influenced by Finney's writings, and it is possible that the dietary aspect of

1   James B. Jordan, *Pig Out? 25 Reasons Why Christians May Eat Pork* (Niceville, FL: Transfiguration Press, 1992) 55–56.

their program can be traced partially to Finney's mediation of the Graham viewpoint."[2] And recent revelations about Gothard tell us how effective *that's* been.

The author of Hebrews tells his readers to stay away from various weird doctrines: "Be not carried about with divers and strange doctrines. For it is a good thing that the heart be established with grace; not with meats, which have not profited them that have been occupied therein" (13:9). Weird doctrines are the kind of thing that carry people about—wafting them here and there. Fads were not a modern development. And it is interesting that the first instance of this kind of thing that comes to his mind is a food fad. And his exhortation draws a bull's-eye on our various food fads, as well. Instead of being wafted by the Bible diet *du jour*, he tells us that the heart should be established by grace, and not by foods. There is a kind of mind that flips this around, and wants the heart to be established by food—wants to be in with God by means of what is put into the mouth. The promises made on behalf of diet spirituality are often extravagant, but they bring no profit to those who are occupied with them. We eat multiple times a day, so someone who is occupied with food fads spends a lot of time on it. But what does he have to show for it? No profit.

2 Ibid.

Once a week I have breakfast with a number of men in our congregation, after an early morning prayer meeting. One of the things we enjoy, apart from fellowship and the food, is giving one another a hard time about the things we order. As I recall, there was quite a bit of discussion about the coconut shavings on oatmeal one time. All in good fun, and is actually an important part of the fellowship. But nobody exhibits the slightest bit of *moral* indignation.

Morality is grounded in religion (and in nothing else), and moral disapproval is therefore at bottom religious disapproval. This is seen in any overdone language that describes food one man gives thanks for as "food pornography" or "feces" and so on. This is a moral and religious disapproval of the eater, who clearly should know better, and it is this kind of disapproval is what I am challenging in this book. Keep in mind that the guy writing this was once hunting around in the bushes for the Korean food that he thought was a rotting cat. Sure, someone else's eating habits might turn your stomach. It's a big world. If our Korean neighbors had offered us some of whatever it was, my response then would probably have been something like, "I don't know, man." I think I would try it now, but it is in highest degree unlikely that I would become a big fan. That's just great.

This is because religious disapproval without clear disapproval from God as recorded in Scripture is legalism *simpliciter*. It is wrong, and it misrepresents what God is like. It is culinary unitarianism. If a man tells me he lost fifty pounds eating nothing but cashews, I will shake his hand and call him a good fellow. If someone tells me that try as he might, he just can't get caviar down, I nod sympathetically. I *can* get it down, but not by much. If someone tells me that mushrooms taste like so many erasers to him, I would urge him to leave them in the bowl for those who can appreciate their hidden excellencies. All these are statements of taste, opinion, or circumstance.

It is when we move from "mushrooms are wasted on me" to "you are a grievous sinner for enjoying mushrooms" that we have crossed the line. And it will not be to the point to write in to say that you are fine with mushrooms because mushrooms are healthy. Let's doctor them until you are not fine with them. Let's fry them up in Crisco, with a splash or two of artificial bacon flavoring.

Wisdom, skill, gratitude and taste all have a role to play in the selection of what's for dinner. *Guilt never does*. (Sure, if you stole your friend's lunch, guilt has a role to play. Work with me here.) Christians who feel guilt over their decisions of what to eat need to go to sleep on the roof, like Peter did, so that they might see the entire inventory of General Mills lowered in a sheet from heaven. If your food is your guilty pleasure, or if your parsimonious disapproval of others is your guilty pleasure, then it is time to bring your kitchen (and all the cupboards therein) to the feet of Christ.

In John 6, the Lord fed the five thousand, and when they thought this was a good reason for making Him king, He got away from them across the water. However, some who found His message for the belly particularly compelling tracked Him down. Jesus told them that they were following Him because of the physical loaves, which was the wrong reason. He told them to work for the food that endures "to everlasting life" (John 6:27). Do not work, He said, for food that perishes. And if we should not work for food that perishes, we shouldn't get worked *up* over food that perishes.

They asked what they needed to do in order to work the works of God. Jesus told them that the work of God is believing in Jesus. In other words, when people believe in Jesus, God is at work. This is not the work we do for God, it is rather the work that God does in us.

They asked for a sign, and since it was getting close to lunchtime, the sign they suggested was manna from Heaven (v. 31). *That* would be a good one, one calculated to keep them interested in theology.

Jesus replied that He was the true food and the true drink, and is given for the life of the world (v. 33). They asked for that bread, not yet understanding what He was talking about (v. 34). Jesus says that He was the true spiritual bread and the true drink, and the one who believes in Him will never go hungry or thirsty. He is speaking of genuine faith because He is speaking of those the Father gives to Him, and they are the ones who will never be cast out (vv. 37–40).

The Jews murmured at this because of what Jesus was claiming to be. Jesus told them not to murmur. He said that everyone who has learned from the Father comes to Him (v. 45). Jesus doubled down on His difficult words, and created additional dissension among the Jews (v. 52). Jesus then went over it yet again (vv. 53–58).

And *that* was the point when He started to lose disciples (v. 60). Jesus said that this was part of the purpose from the beginning (v. 64). This is why He had emphasized that the Father had to give all true disciples (v. 65). "From that time many of his disciples went back, and walked no more with him" (v. 66). Jesus then asked the twelve if they were going too, and Peter replied that they had nowhere to go. Eternal life was with Him (v. 68). Hard teaching like this is a winnowing fan.

Now this is a rich chapter, filled to the top with godly relevance to the entire subject of our contemporary food debates. We need to know how carnal food relates to eternal life. The answer is—not at all. But carnal food is defined as food that is thought of carnally. The sin is never in the food because Jesus declared all foods clean. The sin is always in the sinner. This means that we can sin *with* our food but we cannot sin *by* food.

These people thought carnally of the miraculous food that Jesus had provided, and wanted to make Him king because of it. They also thought of the manna that came down from Heaven carnally. They thought that Jesus should prove Himself that way. The spiritual source of the food didn't keep them from sinning with it.

But when Jesus responded with the undeniable truth that He was the food and drink they needed, and that the mouth that receives this food and drink is the kind of faith the Father gives, He lost a bunch of them. A significant number of His disciples threw up their hands in despair and walked away from Him. Now this was not because Jesus was a lousy communicator. It was because He was a spiritual communicator, and idolaters cannot get their minds around spiritual things. The natural man cannot understand the things of the spirit, because they are spiritually discerned.

Now, here is an obligatory caveat. God doesn't care what kind of food you are eating—tofu or spam from the can—as long as you are eating it with gratitude and peace. "For the kingdom of God is not meat and drink; but righteousness, and peace, and joy in the Holy Ghost" (Rom. 14:17). "For every creature of God is good, and nothing to be refused, if it be received with thanksgiving: For it is sanctified by the word of God and prayer" (1 Tim. 4:4–5). This is actually very simple. And if God doesn't care what food you are eating, so long as you said grace over it sincerely, then I shouldn't care either. And I really don't.

But people often don't believe that I don't care what people eat—because it is convenient for them to keep misconstruing that particular point. The more we talk about granola—which, by the by, I frequently have had for breakfast in the morning, mixed with yogurt, look at me go—the less we are talking about heart attitudes, and relationships between actual people, which are the whole point. But I really enjoy the fact that there are people who eat bird's nest soup.

What a world! And I also enjoy the fact that others eat Campbell's Cream of Chicken soup also, right out of a can, while still others eat yogi fogey soup from the co-op, the main ingredient of which is pure thoughts, locally sourced. All that matters to me is that you like it, are grateful to God while you eat it, and don't have a furrowed brow over it. Just eat your lunch, man!

If you are wound up tight over food—and it doesn't matter in which direction—then the issue is foodolatry. *That* is what the problem is, and not the nature of the food itself.

Now it seems plain to me that our generation has a strange fixation with food. This is not an imaginary problem. Food was given by God to provide us with a recurring occasion for joy, gratitude, and fellowship, and many of us have turned it into a recurring opportunity for fear, shame, and guilt. Can anyone honestly doubt this? Even among Christians, it is common to see people fretting constantly about the levels of toxicity in their bodies courtesy of Certain Corporations (fear), the fattening effects of that entirely unnecessary cheesecake they had at lunch (shame), and the fact that the coffee beans for their mocha were picked by an underpaid laborer in the third world (guilt). On top of this, many Christians want us to mix this fear, shame, and guilt into one big casserole and eat it in the name of Jesus. But Jesus isn't like that. He forgives us our sins, and He does so *entirely independent of whatever it is we are putting in our mouths.*

This terrible mixture of fear, shame and guilt is so prevalent that it is difficult even to see it—but once you see it, you find it everywhere. Fish don't notice how wet they are, and people who think about their colon all the time don't notice that either. This is how idolatry gets into everything—what is the topic of virtually every conversation?

People who are broken by their food issues are not rejected by Jesus for that reason. Whatever your issues are, bring them to Jesus. Don't stop following Jesus. He welcomes all refugees. If you are fleeing from fear, shame and guilt, then come to Him. But if you are a *purveyor* of fear, shame and guilt, you are an apostle of that junk, not a refugee. If you are insistent on everyone feeding everyone something other than Jesus, then you are among those disciples are in the process of departing from Him.

Now given this complicated reality, if someone gives a clarion blast that reveals exactly what is going on, it is hardly to the point to say that quite a few people "didn't understand" what you were saying. That is exactly what happens when you attack this kind of seeping idolatry—people think you need to brush up on your rhetorical skills, they want you to stop mumbling, and they want you to make all your points to the satisfaction of those who have a vested interest in not being satisfied by them. When the apostle Paul preached in Athens—remember, he was one of the greatest minds in the history of the world, and Athens was one of the most idolatrous cities in that same history—he was dismissed as a dilettante, a dabbler, a seed picker (Acts 17:18). "Tear down your idols!" "What did he say? Dare the clown sidles? What kind of sense does *that* make?"

Now some might respond that if we are simply addressing the attitudes only, and not the foodstuffs in themselves, why does it appear that we are focusing most of our attention on "alternativey" stuff? The answer to that is simple. It is the same reason why surfers ride the wave that is headed toward the beach right now, and they never try to ride yesterday's wave in. Yesterday's wave isn't here anymore. There was a time when the up-to-date and most Modern way in Scientific Progress was the idol *du jour*, and it was the hot new thing among regular folks, and it worked in all the same terrible peer pressure ways. And at that time, it was the duty of intelligent pastors to attack all that stuff, *and for all the same reasons*.

In the fifties, if a woman breastfed her baby, she was thought to be acting like a savage, like she wanted to get photographed for *National Geographic* or something. Why didn't she do the *right* thing for her baby and give her this scientific formula in a can? That modernistic hubris really was something—just as bad as the postmodern hubris we are dealing with now.

In the fifties, the woman who breastfed her baby was a woman who got the stink eye. Today it would be the woman who uses formula who gets the stink eye—whether or not she had reasonable grounds for doing so. Now as a pastor *my concern is with the stink eye part*, and not with monitoring how many calories the babies are getting.

But when I deal with bad attitudes, this creates an optical illusion, as though I am taking sides "on the merits" with those who are currently getting the treatment. Not at all—if there were a band of imperialistic formula feeders in my church who were giving major grief to a beleaguered breast feeder, I would admonish them all sharply, so that they might be sound in the faith. And then, having admonished them, I would donate the whole lot of them to the Smithsonian so they could be put into an exhibit.

High-techy modernism is still an idol, but it is now an establishment idol. It doesn't rely on exuberant proselytizing to grow. It doesn't ride on peer pressure (the way it used to). It is just as sinful to bow down to this idol of Science as ever it was, but the idol of Science is not causing tension in the fellowship of the saints the same way that the alternative stuff is currently doing. This is not because of anything inherent in any particular alternative treatment, but rather because as a social movement it is on the ascendant and is growing by proselytizing. The old idol is like a liberal mainstream denominational church, chock full of bad doctrine, but which hasn't proselytized anyone for seventy-five years. But the devotees of new idol are going door-to-door, literature in hand, and are making themselves the topic of conversation.

You can still see the modernist idol at work in television advertisements for the newest Big Pharma drugs. You know the kind—where the fine print ad copy was written by lawyers with a gruesome turn of mind? "Side effects may include writhing on the living room floor, chewing on the coffee table leg, and vomiting up blood." I can't really say I have felt enticed to try MadcowMyrica myself.

Side effects may also include sitting in two claw foot bathtubs in odd, open air locations.

Because the earth is the Lord's (and the fullness thereof), I may take medication my doctor prescribes, and I can do that lawfully, or I might lawfully try something my sister tried and liked. What I may not do in either case is bow down. In other words, there are people who eat things I don't eat, and who treat themselves with medicines that I wouldn't use, who are not in the grip of the problems I am talking about. The thing I am insisting on is that such things ought never to become a barrier to fellowship. That's it. Now, despite this disclaimer, if someone comes up to me angrily and says, "I don't care about all those disclaimers . . . you really are talking about me!" Well, yes, I guess I probably am.

So, then, bring this full circle—back to John 6. There are many people who—because they are not feeding on Christ—are disrupting fellowship over food and medical issues through their imperialism, bad manners, unteachable spirit, insecurity, thoughtlessness, provincialism, and dogmatism.

Here is a composite picture, one I will fill out in greater detail at some other time. Picture a young, married couple with a fairly rocky relationship. She is the one with eighty percent (or more) of the manifesting troubles that they are seeking to resolve. He is being a weak husband (which is not necessarily the same thing as being a weak man), and he supports her fully in her health research and food pursuits because he believes (because of their other recurring conflicts), that he owes her support, and because he thinks a good way to make compensatory peace with her is to have a common foe that they can battle together. She is overwhelmed with her responsibilities with the littles, and gets together regularly with other women who are very much in the same position that she is in—and they talk about their issues a *lot*. The presenting issues become a corporate and social matter this way, and it all spills over into social media. She and her husband are not diligent Bible readers, but to the extent they interact with the Word, they use a way of interpretation that is more a "free association of images" method than it is a "follow the reasoning closely" method. They are not "close" Bible students, and this way of reading Scripture carries over into their way of reading the world. One other symptom is that they have very sloppy entertainment standards that they both share together, and which frequently slops over into a private porn problem that he has.

Now if someone "eats healthy" and that is where the similarity with the preceding paragraph ends, then the reason is simple. None of this is about you, and nobody is upset with what you had for lunch. But the fact it is not about you does not mean that it can't be about anybody. There are many who do fit this description, and the need of the hour is for them to work through John 6 in search of the liberty that is certainly there. And liberty is there because Jesus is there.

But what, someone asks, about Daniel and his three friends? Wasn't the kosher diet they requested healthier *because* it was more moral? Was there a miracle when they refused the king's meat and wine, and came out of a ten-day test healthier than the stable-fed Babylonians?

I believe that this was a matter of Daniel and his friends being faithful to follow the dietary restrictions of the law of Moses. Because they were faithful, God honored their obedience. There are two things I don't believe about this. First, I don't believe that if we could only find out the menu of what they ate back then that we would then have the ultimate "Bible health food." God blesses *obedience*. When He told the Jews to stay away from certain foods, and they did so with a faithful heart, He blessed them. When He tells the Gentiles that all foods are available to us, He honors obedience here just as much. But secondly, I don't believe that honoring obedience needs to involve intervening miracles. The world is a *personal* place, one which God governs through covenantal and providential means. The world is not a machine, where a Gentile in 500 A.D. could get exactly the same results as a Jew eating certain foods in 500 B.C. Nevertheless God governs the world in such a way that His blessings *are* visible.

The second point has to do with the food involved, and the way the Bible describes the results of the competition. For the sake of discussion, let us assume that this really is a creational thing, and that certain foods are health foods in a *biblical* and *spiritual* sense. If we were to embark on an investigation to discover what those foods were, we ought to look for the same results that the Babylonian steward saw in the four faithful Hebrew men.

> "And at the end of ten days their countenances appeared fairer and fatter in flesh than all the children which did eat the portion of the king's meat." (Dan. 1:15)

Their complexions were ruddy and robust, and they had put on a pleasing amount of weight. They won the competition because they were *fatter*. This, in sharp contrast to the current ideal of sallow and scrawny.

One last comment. Suppose someone were to ask why I appear to be so against "healthy eating." First, I have no objection to faithful stewardship when it comes to food, and I do not believe that all foods are equal when it comes to a healthy diet. A steady diet of deep-fried Twinkies is probably not the way to go. If your doctor tells you to knock off the coffee, Ho Hos, and cigars for breakfast, then go ahead and listen to him. But this is a spiritual issue only in terms of stewardship and general wisdom. It is not a case of *spiritual* defilement. People who react to an offered Dorito the way a rabbi would respond to a slice of pork roast *are sinning*. And secondly, as a practical observation, some of the sickliest people I know got that way through an obsessive interest in what they *call* healthy eating, but which obviously isn't. If they were to show up at Melzar's exam after ten days, he would slap them back on the Babylonian diet so fast it wouldn't be funny.

Daniel and his friends were willing to put it to the test. Let's take three groups of kids, and let's look closely at what they eat for ten days. One group watches television constantly, one hand on the remote and the other in a bag of Cheetos. The second group is languishing on a diet of tofu and rice. The last group is fed on what we might call a common sense American mom suburban diet—Honey Nut Cheerios for breakfast, PB&Js for lunch, a couple of cookies after school, and a well-rounded dinner (meat, potatoes, veggies), with a little ice cream for dessert. On the eleventh day, let's have them all run around the block.

Why are we so tempted by these false standards of food righteousness, these overwrought concerns about what we put on our plates or how it got there?

Man is created in the image of God, and however much he wants to deny or negate that image, in this life he cannot do it. For all his efforts, he can only succeed in dislocating it. This means that moral rebellions in one area result in bizarre moralistic crusades in others. This is because man has a need to be visibly righteous. If he is visibly unrighteous in some area that God's moral law plainly and clearly defines, then he must compensate by excessive zeal in "righteousness" elsewhere. But it cannot be righteousness elsewhere as God defines it—for that would be obedience, and the disobedient cannot love obedience.

We live in a generation that has thrown off God's standards of sexual behavior, and because of this, widespread pornography, promiscuity, adultery, blood guilt through abortion and homosexuality have resulted in a vast reservoir of guilt. This guilt is culture-wide, and it is so massive that it has begun to drive and shape the sentiments of everyone, whether or not they are personally guilty. This guilt has to be paid off somehow, and this is one of the central contributions to our current deranged moralism about food.

I think it is really cool that different people cook and eat different foods. I think it is wonderful that some folks grow their own, and it is most excellent that other people get their food out of cans and boxes. When it comes to food choices, I think catholic and eclectic is good—live and let live, eat and let eat. What I can't abide is moralism about food. In the absence of any word from God on it, it would be wisdom on our part to keep quiet about what we see on the other fellow's fork. But we don't. We legislate for others, and make censorious faces at them. We launch crusades.

In short, a sexually guilty people have accepted as "normal" the most unnatural practices imaginable, and they have then demanded that their food be "all natural." Wisdom is vindicated by her children. This guilt-driven desire has resulted in an entire industry springing up that caters to the deep desire that a morally inferior people have to feel morally superior. That's hard to do, and so there's money to be made there if you pull it off. You have to pick something out at random, and then make people bad for deviating from the new arbitrary norm.

The food thing is a subset of the whole ecochondriac mania. To take one hilarious example, on planet Earth, which is mostly water, we are in a panic over running out of water. Otherwise educated people are in all of a doodah. We think we are depleting the aquifer (whichever aquifer near you is being depleted) by watering the lawn, we think we are saving the planet by putting a brick in the flush tank of the toilet, and we turn our water off and on while brushing our teeth in order to feel that warm glow of self-congratulation. But I got off of food righteousness and got onto water righteousness. Anything for some folks but Bible righteousness.

Back to food. Even some Christians have been caught up in this bogus moralism generated by these guilty people, and have come to believe that this is a "stewardship" issue. But it is only a stewardship issue if stewards are allowed to depart entirely from the instructions left for them in their master's written instructions. It is only a stewardship issue if men are allowed to create their own morality apart from Scripture. Where does Scripture tell us to beware of industrialized food chains? Just curious.

And the people who are morally indignant about industrialized food chains are the same ones whose definitions of "natural" change radically as we move from the dining room to the bed room. If all the food-ist people who were living in ongoing sexual disobedience had a heart attack one day (because, as it happens, little known fact, tofu causes heart disease), the whole hipster food industry would collapse, and the "stewardship" Christians would find out that their stewardship movement had been subsidized the whole time by moralistic scam artists. And they would further discover that old fashioned steward-ship, the kind the Bible talks about, would start look-ing sideways at the three-dollar apples, now that they weren't deemed cool any more. Because, as it turns out, the coolness factor had been created and sus-tained by guilt, and now that the guilty had all gone to their tofu-deaths, those remaining would have a lot of rethinking to do.

Take the moralistic condemnation of others away, and there is nothing wrong with whatever you might want to eat. Suit yourself, and thank God for what-ever is on your plate. But you can only thank God for whatever food is there if there is no self-righteousness in your heart. Take that moralistic condemnation of others away, and it also turns out that eating a bunch of this stuff isn't that much fun anymore. The party, it seems, was elsewhere.

> Wherefore if ye be dead with Christ from the ru-diments of the world, why, as though living in the world, are ye subject to ordinances, (Touch not; taste not; handle not; Which all are to perish with the using;) after the commandments and doctrines

> of men? Which things have indeed a shew of wisdom in will worship, and humility, and neglecting of the body; not in any honour to the satisfying of the flesh. (Col. 2:20–23)

The prohibitionist streak that is so attractive to many Christians is a religious streak. And we must come to understand that this religious streak goes as deep as the flesh does. There is a kind of religious duty that is of the flesh, for the flesh, and by the flesh.

We do not have to reconstruct the particular rationale for the prohibitions that the Colossians were having to deal with. What we have to do is simply recognize that there is something like this out there in the world, in the religious world, and in the religious heart. There are certain practices which will have the appearance of wisdom for Christians, but which are of no value in actually dealing with the flesh. This is because this kind of asceticism does not mortify the flesh—it *is* the flesh. This is why anyone serious about the Christian life will want to guard himself against falling into this particular kind of trap. The traps that have the appearance of wisdom are the camouflaged ones. This means they are the ones to watch out for. There is this kind of trap? What should I watch for?

In the coming verses, in chapter three of Colossians, the apostle will be urging them to their real duties of mortification. But what he wants them to put to death are those deeds related to "fornication, uncleanness, inordinate affection, evil concupiscence, and covetousness, which is idolatry" (Col. 3:5). If you are wondering anything like "whatever could he mean?" you might start by swearing off all movies that are anything like the last twenty movies you watched.

This is why all hipster mortifications are so lame. The apostle saith nothing whatever about carbon footprints, shade grown coffee, ethical chickens, corporate farming—all that moral earnestness being wasted with such prodigal abandon! Did you know that we are just 5 percent of the world's population, and yet we still consume 62 percent of the world's priggishness?

Boycottery

Many years ago, when we were first learn-ing how to handle our weapons in the culture wars, I had to sort through what I thought about boycotts. And where I landed is related to a point that has continuing relevance for Christians who are trying to sort out how to relate to the broader culture. I concluded at that time that boycotting is a tactic, and not a moral imperative. Sometimes it is a wise tactic, and sometimes it is foolishly employed, but we are not obligated to refrain from something because of where it came from or where it is going. We are allowed to boycott something in the hope of getting something valuable done. We are not obligat-ed to boycott something for the sake of maintaining

51

our own moral purity. This applies to gas stations that sell porn, to motel chains owned by Mormons, and to your small box of Chicken McNuggets. Many years ago my wife got a panicked phone call from a woman who had heard that Proctor & Gamble had an occult logo, and that their CEO had appeared on some television show or other to declare that their profits went to Satan. My response to this (false) rumor was to say that if Satan had indeed changed vocations and moved over into soap manufacturing, that this should be thought by all of us to be all to the good. Boycott? Rather, shouldn't we push this along?

There are two objections to this neomonastic ideal—separation for the sake of purity—and both objections are fatal. The first is that it is an impossible ideal. What can't be done won't be done. Serious attempts at even partial consistency here will result in nothing but paralysis—and paralysis is not cultural engagement. If we are contaminated by what is done with our money after it leaves our hands, or by the history of the product we are purchasing before it reaches our hands, then all of us are contaminated all the time, all the way. On that calculus, name one clean thing in this sorry world.

The second objection is that the Bible flatly prohibits this kind of moral fussiness:

All things are lawful for me, but all things are not expedient: all things are lawful for me, but all things edify not. Let no man seek his own, but every man another's wealth. Whatsoever is sold in the shambles, that eat, asking no question for conscience sake: For the earth is the Lord's, and the fullness thereof. If any of them that believe not bid you to a feast, and ye be disposed to go; whatsoever is set before you, eat, asking no question for conscience sake. But if any man say unto you, This is offered in sacrifice unto idols, eat not for his sake that shewed it, and for conscience sake: for the earth is the Lord's, and the fullness thereof: Conscience, I say, not thine own, but of the other: for why is my liberty judged of another man's conscience? For if I by grace be a partaker, why am I evil spoken of for that for which I give thanks? Whether therefore ye eat, or drink, or whatsoever ye do, do all to the glory of God. (1 Cor. 10:23–31)

God owns everything—not Satan, not the Mormons, and not Tyson Chicken. Something can have been offered up to some Baal or other in a cloud of pagan smoke, and the meat still remains the Lord's. The history of the meat does nothing to inject demonic influences into it. It would still be appropriate to say some kind of wholesome Norman Rockwell grace over it.

Paul is very plain here that we are to do everything to the glory of God, whether we eat or drink. But he tells us to do this in a manner that makes it very clear that we should be able to do this with a well-salted French fry, deep fried in something icky. If I am spending some time at lunch with a weaker brother (for that is what he is), I would pick him up a sandwich from the Food Co-op, and would not bring him a small tub of pump cheese fries from DeathMart. I would do this for conscience's sake—his, not mine. The reason I wouldn't do it for *my* conscience's sake is that we are not allowed to have our liberty judged by the fussers and the scruplers. Love dictates that you refrain from waving something obnoxious under the nose of a brother with scruples about it. Christ died for him, so you may not do that (Rom. 14:15). At the same time, we need to reject, and reject with godly vehemence, every attempt to bind the consciences of the saints with regard to what they may eat (Col. 2:20–23). We defer to the weaker brothers at lunch, which is not the same thing as letting them teach on this.

How do some brothers develop such weaknesses, anyway?

When an insecure third grader wants to be accepted by his schoolmates, and he is afraid that they will see and identify his lowly origins, by which he means his folks and the rest of his family, the way he tries to insinuate himself into the good graces of the cool set that he wants to impress is by making fun of (or distancing himself from) his own people first. The maneuver is perfectly transparent to everyone outside the peculiar dynamics involved, and perfectly invisible to those in the grip of it. But for those who want to know what is going on, disloyal insecurity would be one way to put it. Insecure disloyalty would be another.

What does this have to do with food? Nothing, actually, not with food as such. But it does have something to do with the hunger to be hip that afflicts (a stronger word would do) a particular quadrant of the evangelical world, which is searching in vain for a way to look like they are standing up for biblical faith while they are in fact capitulating to the very latest forms of unbelief. The hunger to be culturally engaged and cool is the driving force behind evangelical calls for stewardship—whether it might be stewardship of high priced produce or the weather we seem to be having. Stewardship is cool, unless of course, you try to be a steward on behalf of unborn children or biblical monogamy.

There are all kinds of legit reasons that can be appealed to as we make our food choices. Cost (up or down), taste, challenge, fun, romance, color and so forth can all enter into it. And there is no reason to be egalitarian. There are superior forms of farming, transport, selling and cooking of food, just as there are better ways to harvest the hard wood for the making of superior cabinets. There is such a thing as superior cooking period, as can be seen in a high end restaurant, as compared with the ministrations of a third rate hash slinger manfully wielding a skillet in a back room of a diner off I-90 in rural somewhere. There is such a thing as superior comfort food, which can be seen in the kind of mac and cheese my mom used to make and my wife now makes, and there is mac and cheese that is burned on the bottom by some enemy of humanity. There is corn on the cob that was picked and shucked ten minutes ago, and popped in the boiling water, and there is corn on the cob that was harvested in the days of Edward the Confessor. And let us say that the butter you put on the fresh corn was butter you churned yourself, right before you picked the corn. Who but a Philistine would object to the delights that are involved?

And who but a Pharisee would connect any of this to spirituality, or moral superiority? We live in a country where the unborn are still routinely slaughtered, and homos are married off like nothing unusual was happening. Whether the grain in my bread spent too much time in a truck somewhere in Wyoming is a moral consideration that is clean off my radar. Like, who cares?

> Now the Spirit speaketh expressly, that in the latter times some shall depart from the faith, giving heed to seducing spirits, and doctrines of devils; Speaking lies in hypocrisy; having their conscience seared with a hot iron; Forbidding to marry, and commanding to abstain from meats, which God hath created to be received with thanksgiving of them which believe and know the truth. For every creature of God is good, and nothing to be refused, if it be received with thanksgiving: For it is sanctified by the word of God and prayer. (1 Tim. 4:1–5)

So what, exactly, can be sanctified by the word of God and prayer? A list would include, but not be limited to, escargot, homegrown cantaloupe, grilled steak, chicken strips and jojos from the supermarket deli, sharp cheddar, Safeway cantaloupe, those cool little Japanese crackers with the seaweed on them, bread—all kinds, a double Whopper with cheese and onions, trout the way my chef friend Francis prepares it, hand cranked ice cream, ice cream that was squirted into a carton by a machine that cost three million dollars, corn on the cob, bacon, eggs, bacon grease, eggs cooked in bacon grease, ginger snaps with Stilton cheese on them, red red wine, home-made croutons, and Caesar salad adorned with the aforementioned croutons. One should get the drift, although many unfortunately do not.

So what does it take to sanctify a plate full of stuff that comes to us through the industrial food chain? A grateful, overflowing heart, lifting the word of God and prayer over it. Then open your eyes (and heart) and reach for the fork. There are no cooties in the cupboard. They've been exterminated by the perfectly organic pesticide of thankfulness.

CHAPTER 4

Poison and Medicine

Ronald Deutsch aptly described one aspect of our problematic attitude toward food. He referred to "the perennial complication"—everybody thinks *they're* the authority on the connections between eating and health. We are so sure of our vilification of some foods as poisonous and our veneration of others as medicinal that it can be pretty difficult to get across any point to the contrary.[3] But I will try.

As for the "poison" objection, it is true that a man could bow his head to say grace over a meal that has been poisoned and that will still kill him dead. If he eats, he is not spiritually sinning in any way, but he *is* going

---

3 Ronald Deutsch, *The New Nuts Among the Berries* (Palo Alto, CA: Bull Publishing, 1977).

to be physically harmed. Surely I am not arguing that poison is okay? Right, I am not. Poison is not okay, and intentionally ingesting it is, at best, bad stewardship.

My answer to this objection is that we are now debating a question of fact, and moral indignation simply gets in the way of the discussion. If this is poison, surely it is a very *odd* kind? My whole life I have been ingesting poisons that my great-great-grandfather never, ever encountered, and taking the averages I will probably live thirty to forty years longer than he did. To this a reply could be made that there are many other variables and if I hadn't been eating those poisons I would have out-lasted him by sixty instead of a mere thirty, but this seems to me to slip away from the standard definition of poison. You don't slip someone poison in order to slightly retard the progress of his galloping and ever-burgeoning health. Poison kills people, plunk. It doesn't issue mild admonitions so that the health is careful not to get too proud. That's not poison. Put another way, all these other variables, granting their existence, make it reasonable for a ninety-year-old man, who has been eating at MacDonald's since they first came out, to believe that he was not poisoned, not *successfully* at any rate.

Let me make a modest observation: There is no such *thing* as a poison. By this I mean that nothing is harmful to the human body in small enough amounts, and everything is harmful in large enough amounts. Different substances vary in potency, to be sure, so that some things will reach dangerous levels of toxicity sooner than others, but nothing is harmful in itself. Everything depends on frequency and amount. Use your head, and don't panic just because you read a scientific name for something on the label.

I am given to understand that apple seeds have cyanide in them. If you eat apples as I sometimes do, core and all, you are ingesting cyanide. If you grind the whole thing up in a cider mill to be organic and healthy-like, you are feeding your family cyanide. And all this is no problem whatever. Yay for cyanide. But if you saved the seeds from a bushel of apples, and then ate them all at once, then you would have a pretty big problem. Now, are apple seeds "poison" or not? Do apples have a poisonous center?

But to think about amounts, frequency, ratios and so forth is far too complicated for those who want the world of food and health to be *simple*. This is the mentality that wants to know if any "chemicals" are in the food or not. Well, what's the alternative?

And lest this be taken as a mistake made only by health nut rubes, it should be added that whenever an agency like the FDA pronounces a particular substance suspect, the chances are good that this mistake is lurking in the background. You see, what they did was take the substance in question (something found, for example, in diet cola), and they fed it to lab rats in such amounts that the cases had to be brought into their testing center with forklifts. Well, if I drank fifty-two cases of Dr Pepper a day for three months running, I would be astonished if I *didn't* get cancer.

Jordan notes the standard of healthiness that we ought to be most concerned about, but are most likely to neglect: "*The key to health is obedience and faith, not mechanical observance of health techniques.* Valuable as exercise, good diet, and the like may be, they are not delineated in God's revealed law."[4]

Among the informal logical fallacies, one of the most common is called the *post hoc ergo propter hoc* fallacy. Translated it means "after this, therefore because of this." B follows A, and it is therefore assumed that A must have been the cause of B. This fallacy is so prevalent that it could easily be assumed that many have done graduate studies in it, and some have even moved on to *post hoc* post doc work.

The problem is complicated because B frequently is caused by A. God placed us in a world where we see cause and effect happening all the time. But for

4   Jordan, *Pig Out?*, 58.

every antecedent real cause there is a multitude of antecedent non-causes. I am about to type the letter t—there!—and this was caused by my left index finger pushing on a key with a t on it. But at the very same moment, there were a bunch of objects on my desk that were not pushing that key, along with numerous objects in the world that were not doing it either. In order to cause something, more is necessary than to simply exist prior to that event.

But sometimes the events that are not "causing it" occur in such a way that it is reasonable to assume that they might have. This is where a lot of *post hoc* thinking comes in. You eat at a particular restaurant, order the salmon, and two hours later you fall deathly ill. Even if you find out later that it was the flu and had nothing to do with the salmon, it might be years—depending on how sick you got—before you can even look at salmon, or go to that restaurant. In other words, even our bodies have a strong tendency to argue *post hoc*. Mark Twain once said that a cat that sits on a hot stove plate will never sit on a hot stove plate again—but neither will it sit on a cold one.

All this appears to be a design feature, and quarreling with it is just sweeping water uphill. But God did not just give us the power of association, He also gave us the power of thought. "Maybe it was something I ate" is a reasonable question. Connecting various possible associations is indeed a rational way to form hypotheses. It is an incoherent way to draw conclusions. A reasonable man ought wonder if he is allergic to this or that if he constantly reacts with a rash whenever he eats it. That question ought to lead to some kind of experimentation and thoughtful research. If he wonders if he is lactose intolerant, for another example, then it reasonable to knock off the dairy for a bit and see what happens. Read up on it. Talk to a doctor.

What is not reasonable is to wonder if that is the case, listen to a friend who diagnosed himself with the same condition, note a couple of similarities, read one article on the Internet about it (at TrustworthyAnswers.com) and form a dogmatic opinion that will then be defended to the last ditch. What this approach will result in is a Christian community full of allergies, half of which are genuine and half of which are not, and a host of table fellowship issues.

If you are invited over to someone's house and you bring your own food because, you say, "I'm a picky eater," this is what would be called indefensible. So nobody does that. It has to be cloaked in medical garb—"I have allergies"—and that way everybody has to leave you alone.

So that no one will think I am writing about them in particular, let me make an example up. And let us also be honest. If I had not told you that I was making it up, you would have had to Google it to find out. These are difficult days in which to be a satirist. And who knows? Maybe you will Google it anyway, and discover that I made up a treatment that somebody else made up too, only he's making some money off it.

Suppose you scotch tape a Cheerio to your forehead overnight to discover whether you have any grain allergies. Suppose further you misjudge your audience the next day, and as you are telling them about your discoveries in alternative science, somebody objects to your methods and procedures. He blurts out, before reflecting on the social niceties, that that's kinda stupid.

You have had to deal with criticism before, and so you reply with a stock answer from the warehouse—"you know, the Bible says that we are fearfully and wonderfully made." This is quite true. The Bible does say that. But when we think about the track record of the web site you got this unique diagnostic approach from, we might also come to the conclusion that you were fearfully and wonderfully *had*—especially if you paid ready money to have FedEx ship you

the Cheerio. The human body is fearfully and wonderfully made (Ps. 139:14), sure. The brain is fearfully and wonderfully made, too, which seems to be an
invitation to all of us to use it a bit more.

The issue is not whether we can get odd medicines
from odd places. Who knew that squid spleen could
cure that rash? The issue is not whether we can get
odd allergic reactions to odd combinations of stuff.
We are, after all, fearfully and wonderfully made. It is
a crazy world, and crazy things can happen.

The issue concerns the laws of logic, and how
you go about verifying something. The issue is
not whether a Cheerio could be able to tell you
something. The issue is whether you go through a
thoughtful process of elimination or not. The issue
is whether your thesis is falsifiable in any reasonable
way. The issue is whether or not you know why it
should be falsifiable.

Superstition is not knowledge. Wouldn't-it-be-nice
research is not research. Dispensing with the laws of
orderly thought is not knowledge. One of the things
that the Reformed faith has done well over the course
of centuries is that it has encouraged believers to love
the Lord their God with all their *minds*. One of the
more discouraging developments in recent years is
the spectacle of superstitious epistemologies making

their way back into our churches. The reason I write so forcefully on this subject is that I am allergic to this kind of thinking. How do I know? I taped one of them to my forehead and got a rash.

CHAPTER 5

Natural & Organic versus Chemical & Corporate

A ll systems of thought have terms of praise
and blame. In the world of the new food, a
central term of praise is the word *natural*.
It is only natural, therefore, that we take a look at it.

A particular food is described as "natural," or perhaps even "all-natural." We all know enough to know
that this is supposed to be taken as a good thing, but
what does it mean exactly?

There are a series of questions that I think we need
to work through. First, what does it mean to say that
a food is natural? Secondly, does this food in fact
match that description? Third, if it does in fact match
that description, is it good or bad? In short, what are

we talking about, is this what we are talking about, and if it is, does it matter?

Let us walk through this process with one variable. Is it natural to cook food? Once we have answered that question, we can ask if this food is cooked. And last, we may ask if it is bad to eat cooked food, whether it is natural or not. The first question defines the term, the second applies the definition to a particular food, and the last asks whether natural is an appropriate term of praise in this instance.

Some of these questions are harder than they look. In fact, all of them are. What is "natural" about baking bread? If we grind grain for the flour, how much artifice is allowed? Is it natural to cook oats that are whole, but unnatural to cook oats that are rolled? You are doing something extra (to release nutrients) when you roll them, but is that bad? Human ingenuity is being applied to the oats, but we are also doing that when we put them in a pot on the stove. Going back to the bread, in order to be natural do we have to eat the grain the way Christ's disciples did, rubbing the grain in their hands?

But suppose we get past this hurdle, and we have defined natural as something culled from nature, and not too much fooling around with it either. Let us say that we have also defined "fooling around," limiting it to six steps at the factory. Now take the example of pure vanilla and its nearly identical sister vanillin. What is the difference between them? One is the extract of an orchid bean and the other is extracted from wood pulp. The problem is that wood is every bit as natural and organic as the orchid bean is. So you have to put artificial vanilla on that bottle, but in what sense is it artificial? The artifice that is applied is no different in kind than the artifice applied to the orchid bean.

Another great example is petroleum. There's a natural product for you—right out of the ground, from the bosom of mother nature. Boil it off and you get sugars, and then flavor chemists can tinker with it and get you some stupendous flavorings that will take you back to strawberry fields forever. Suppose that the flavor chemists stayed within their allotted number of steps, such that we could not say they were fooling around. Is this natural?

Now suppose we have defined natural, and defined the limited number of steps to keep a product natural. We have determined that this particular product falls within that stipulated definition. Poisonous mushrooms can fit within the definition, and almond-flavored petroleum sugars won't. And yet, the former will kill you dead, and the latter will top off your birthday ice cream, and make that day complete. Natural kills.

Unnatural delights. Perhaps natural is a singularly bad word to describe what is good for us. And yet it is a word that is sought out and used by many because it leaves a *lot* of room for fuzzy thinking. Every time I see something advertised as "all natural and free of chemicals" I brace myself for the day—and it cannot be far off now—when certain food items are touted on the package as being entirely "molecule free."

In sum, natural food that is genuinely natural is very hard to define. Once defined, it is hard to categorize various food without becoming arbitrary (which governmental agencies are good at). What would you call a bottle of orchid vanilla (80 percent) mixed with wood pulp vanillin (20 percent). What is that, besides being 100 percent organic? And last, once we have all this sorted out, we are no closer to knowing what is healthy for us.

This means that when I am lectured about the importance of eating natural, I feel like I am being urged, with great importunity, to remain in the western hemisphere. Can we narrow this down a bit?

And so this explains why, when harangued, I do not run off. I just sit there, like a scolded cat.

This common use of the word *natural* as an unqualified term of praise reflects a failure to apply the doctrine of the Fall to life around us.

First, the doctrine. God created the world and all that it contains, and behold, it was all very good. When our first parents rebelled against Him, the created order fell along with the lords of that created order. That which was previously good was now a *damaged* good. The creation was subjected to futility and bondage to decay. But God promised a Savior who would, in the fullness of time, restore everything in such a way that the world would be made new. The gospel is the message in which we proclaim this good news, and Christians are those who look forward to this coming restoration. So the basic Christian message is one of creation, fall, and redemption. That redemption is ongoing in an already/not yet fashion, but will not be complete until the day of resurrection.

Now this means that we cannot point to *anything* in the created order and justify its use in a particular way simply on the basis of its being "natural." Nor can we reject anything on the basis of it having been "processed." The creation around us is a damaged good, and this means that when we point to a particular aspect of it, we are not yet clear whether we are pointing to an aboriginal good, or to one of the defects introduced by the Fall. When we approach a particular food for the first time, knowing nothing about it other than that it is "natural," we still don't know if it is good or bad, healthy or unhealthy. A worm-ridden apple is natural. And the same thing goes for processed foods. It could be good or bad, healthy or unhealthy, *depending*. Because God has commanded us to exercise dominion in a world where those who are to exercise dominion are participants in the Fall, this means that we can screw it up. So then, natural is not automatically good or bad. Processed is not automatically good or bad.

I used the word *apply* earlier. I am not saying that Christians who blithely assume that "natural is good" are denying the doctrine of the Fall. I am saying that they are not *applying* it. It does not factor into their thinking the way it ought to. Rousseau gave us the idea that returning to a state of innocence was possible and desirable. But since then, whenever we have tried it, the results have been particularly problematic. False doctrine does not lead the way to true living. It is not possible to ignore the fact that we are a fallen race in a fallen creation, and to have that ignorance be without consequence.

Here is an example that is not about food directly, but it still illustrates the point well. "Natural childbirth" is a very common way of refusing to apply the doctrine of the Fall, ignoring the curse that God placed upon childbearing. To say that pregnancy is not a disease is quite true. To say that giving birth is a natural process is quite true also. But this overlooks the fact that it is a *cursed* natural process. Eve was given turmoil in the bearing of children, just as Adam was given weeds in the garden.

The weeds in my garden grow naturally. The cold virus multiplies naturally. Cancer cells develop naturally, and occupy their place in the ecosystem of the human body.

Now the response to all this might be to say that if we have a robust doctrine of the Fall, then should we not be suspicious of sweeping claims (from fallen humans) to be able to "improve," or "enrich," or "develop"? Certainly, we should. Not every claimed improvement really is. The doctrine of the Fall should apply there as well, and in fact, it *must* apply there. But we are not measuring this faulty exercise of dominion over against "the natural state." As we look at nature, we are looking at something which needs to be cultivated and improved in some ways, and left alone in others. *We cannot find out which is which from nature herself.* In the cultural mandate (which the Fall did not abrogate) mankind was given the responsibility to exercise dominion, which is to say, man is the one who is responsible to dig, cultivate, prune, spray, let alone, etc. as appropriate. Because we are sinners, and because we have not yet reached the maturity in Christ we ought to have, there will be times when we leave the tree alone when we ought to have sprayed, and there will be times when we spray when we ought not to have. Sure. But our task is to learn from our mistakes, and to grow up in Christ.

But Christ and His Word are the standard, *not nature*. Nature is the canvas—not the painting manual. Nature is not and cannot be the standard. Christ and what He reveals are the standard, and this includes what He reveals in nature. But while autonomous nature is not the standard, nature as a created thing can reveal certain things about God. All of this is to say that something is not good to eat simply because it was found "in nature," or is "all natural."

And everything I have said about nature goes double for *organic*. Not to mention that certain pesky scientists have shown that organic food isn't any more nutritional than the kind that has had the bugs sprayed off.[5]

But all is not lost. We can still feel superior, which is the thing we are fundamentally hungry for. Organic food production is much better on the climate change front, which, come to think of it . . . 1) we don't know

---

5 For a summary of one such study, see Jessica Daly, "Study: Organic food not more nutritional," CNN International, http://edition.cnn.com/2008/TECH/science/08/19/organic.cooking.pv/index.html (accessed Aug. 29, 2016).

is happening anyway; 2) we don't know we are causing it even if it is happening; 3) we don't know we can
do anything about it even if we are causing it; and 4)
we don't know that it is a bad thing, or that we ought
to be doing anything about it, even if we are causing
it. But organic farming is helping fight that climate
change battle anyway, and yay for our team.

So those Christians who use "natural" and "organic" as terms of praise, and who eschew the use of
"chemicals" in food preparation are failing at three
places. First, as I have noted, they are not applying the doctrine of the Fall. They are not capable of
finding any food in this world that has an unfallen
nature, for which natural would work as a term of
unqualified praise. Second, they are not able to find
a food anywhere that is not made out of chemicals.
Chemical-free food would a sight to behold, and a
miracle in its own right. And third, they are giving
weight, and moral weight, at that, to standards that
have little to do with objective value and much to do
with marketing. In the first instance, they are not really thinking in Christ. In the second and third, they
are just following along with popular jargon and not
really thinking at all.

Jargon has a tendency to distract us from paying
careful attention to basic logic—a much needed thing

in our discussions about contemporary foodism. Related to this is the careless use of certain terms that are not defined as they ought to be, and are not used consistently thereafter.

Whenever we are beat up with jargon, we don't really learn what the debate is actually over. If someone were stridently opposed to what I am willing to put into my mouth, and I asked him *why*, we are not going to get very far if his objection is that my food is made up of molecules. So is his food, and so now what do we do?

When someone objects to "chemical additives" but loudly applauds "nutritional supplements," we should be forgiven if we believe that some obfuscatory hand-waving is going on. Now, please note that I am not saying that all chemical additives are good or that all nutritional supplements are bad. I am saying that, so far as our definitions have gone, *they are the same thing*, some of them good and some of them bad. Nothing is bad because a factory put it in a bottle, and nothing is good for the same reason.

Discussions on this subject are plagued with this kind of thing. Objections are commonly made, for example, to the fact that the shelves of our grocery stores are stocked by "food corporations." Okay. Who stocks the shelves at Whole Foods? No corporations,

I hope? No big business, I trust? And I *sincerely* hope that no money changes hands.

And who stocks the mini-Whole Foods tucked away inside a Safeway near you? Not corporate entities with a budget anything over a million a year, let us hope? For, as we all know, that kind of thing would be inherently corrupting.

When I hear people discussing this kind of thing, I frequently hear words used disparagingly of one kind of food, or in praise of another kind, and for all I can make out, the words apply in equal measure and in the same ways to both alternatives. This bacon cheeseburger is full of molecules.

This is not to say that there are no real differences in food choices, but rather that in popular discussions, a good portion of the energy is spent on scrambling for a right to use the good words for oneself, and the bad words on the eating habits of the other side. This is like one presidential candidate saying that his opponent would be a disaster for the nation because he stands behind wood lecterns at debates, with this salient point being made from behind a wood lectern at a debate. No, it is not like that, because if this happened at a presidential debate, everyone would be howling with laughter. When it happens (as it does, all the time) on the subject of natural food, everybody just sits there, solemn as a judge. *Chemicals*? Really?

"Food corporations"—so is natural and organic farming big business or not? "Factories"—do those green and healthy-looking tortilla chips make themselves? "Pills"—but only pills with chemicals in them are bad and those with nutrients in them are good. Glad that's settled. "Factory farming"—when the demand for real healthy milk gets up to the gazillion-dollar-a-year level, which should be any day now, I will be really interested to visit the dairy farms that will no doubt be right there to meet this demand, and to take careful note of the ways in which such operations do not resemble factory farming. "Health food"—a bit like one Christian saying that he attends a "Spirit-filled church," wondering what kind *you* attend.

These are words that are being used to obscure. Scripture requires equal weights and measures. If one side gets corporations, then so does the other. If one side doesn't get to have them, then the other side can't either.

And if I may make an important point in passing, if anyone seriously thinks that by going natural, he will be escaping The Establishment, finally getting away from The Man and from the clutches of the food corporations, I have a bit of bad news. The corporations are *way* ahead of you. There are high-powered boards sitting around half-an-acre mahogany tables on the thirty-third floors of skyscrapers in New York City, and they are meeting right this minute, and they are making decisions on the marketing of the ponderosa pine bark chips, lightly salted. If you slice them thin enough, they approach being edible. We are long past the point where the money involved in all this caught the attention of the "food corporations." The Man knows all about you and your penchant for dinners that are synchronized with the rhythms of the earth. The Man likes your penchants. He is there to *serve* them. And he doesn't in the least mind when they are inconsistent.

Advertisers and mass marketers have figured out that there are a lot of people out there who are like sheep without a shepherd. They want to prod and steer everybody into various purchases and brand loyalties, and they industriously work at it. This is something we *should* respond to, but my suggested response would not be to say that people have to choose between Ads and Adbusters, between corporate and fake alternative corporate.

Protesting the new global economy and actually escaping it are two different things.

My response has been to encourage the establishment of Christian schools that teach kids how to think like Christians, how to identify fallacies, how to stand up to group-think, and so on. Nothing is more truly counter-cultural than holiness. There is nothing new about any of this—the choice is the same in every generation, and that choice is holiness or the world. There is nothing new under the sun, including the lie that there actually is something new.

So we must not trust in worldly alternatives to the world. That just gets us opting into secular right/left divisions, or becoming a Laurelist instead of a Hardyist. And we can't fix things by opting for a thin Christian veneer of these right/left distinctions—Sean Hannity or N.T. Wright.

So in trying to lean against this problem of thoughtless brand loyalty, I don't want to trust the critical outlook of people who would stand in line for three days for the latest iPhone. They might not know what the actual problem is, and so perhaps we should call them iPhoneys.

Full disclosure: I do own an iPhone myself, but I have managed to do this without being one of the cool kids. The issue is not the *thing*, but rather our approach to the thing. Same as with food. Our temptation is to objectify the problem, trying to locate sin in the stuff—in the tobacco, in the alcohol, in the gun, in the donut—instead of where sin is actually located, which is right under the breastbone.

A fancy resort hotel a bit north of us here offers their rich clientele botox treatments on a walk-in basis. Now let us assume we have got ourselves four fake-baked platinum blonde types with eight silicone implants between them, and the girls all decide to go in for some of the available botox treatments, and so they make a party of it. *That* important task accomplished, they all decide to go out for lunch. We follow them to an up-scale fern bistro to see what they are having. Now I have twenty dollars here that says all four of them order a salad with twigs in it because eating "natural" is important to them. Now am I the only one in the world who thinks that there is *something* in our culture's approach to "all natural" that is seriously demented?

Now please note. I am *not* saying that everyone who wants to "eat healthy" is motivated this way, or is "seriously demented." Of course not. If you live in Boulder, Colorado, or Santa Cruz, California, and you want to stay alive, you pretty much have to eat this way—yogi or nothing. However, I *am* saying that the fact that a lot of this kind of faddishness-on-plate is largely invisible to a large number of people means something, and that something is not good.

Okay, to sum up. We are choosing (generally) between two different styles of lifestyle eating. Both involve manufactured and processed foods that have passed through factories, and they all have chemicals in them. All the factories are owned by corporations. What do we do now?

A former student suggested to me that the answer lies in a return to a more agrarian approach. He granted that there is no sin per se in eating a Big-Mac, etc., non-idolatrously wondered if there were "simple Christian wisdom in the pre-modern way of doing things." He expanded:

> Put another way, Should we as Christians, in the establishment of a new culture, a Christ-centered one, be proactive in finding ways that circumvent the current paradigm of highly industrialized and highly processed foods?
>
> Should our desires for wholeness and beauty and gratitude toward both our Maker and His creation (i.e., toward one another) drive us away from these highly complicated, government-dictated food systems? Should we not, in the main, be pursuing the type of food cultures (sans idolatry) found in the farmers' markets, with their chickens that are treated like chickens, and the cattle given food they were created to eat, and vegetables grown in a way that is consistent with

the way God created things to grow, (i.e., sunlight
and water)?

These were all great questions, and I think they reveal precisely why Christians find the new food movement attractive in so many ways. In short, how could
someone like Chesterton and not like farmers' markets?

I agree we should be "proactive in finding ways
that circumvent the current paradigm." But I would
argue that the foodist reaction to industrial farming
is *part* of the current paradigm, part of what must be
rejected. This reaction (that is part of the paradigm)
is found not just in the idolatrous value they place on
their practices, but also in the practices themselves. I
don't go into a debate between an industrial farmer
and an organic farmer with the assumption that the
organic farmer is right with regard to the substance
of the dispute, though he may be unduly attached
to that right. His attachments may have clouded his
judgment, and not just his values. The same thing
goes for the industrial farmer. I don't assume him to
be in the right either.

In other words, I don't think we can just adopt
the standards of the organic movement, while (non-
idolatrously) keeping those standards in an appropriate place in the hierarchy of values. Idols do
more than rearrange standards; they also *generate*

standards. Thus I should always ask, "Is this right?" and not just "Is this too important?"

For example, "all natural" is now a term of praise, but it is a phrase that brings a set of standards along with it. Are those standards correct? Where did they come from? Why is natural good? Who says? Who is the keeper of the "natural" measuring stick, and how much did he pay for it? Is the government involved? And is *natural* an accurate claim, even assuming the standard to be correct? In other words, suppose *all natural* is swell— printing *all natural* on the label doesn't make anything happen, other than clinching a sale to the gullible.

In the fifties, "enriched" was a term of praise. The manufacturer was promising you that they did not just bake the loaf of bread and put it a bag—oh, no. They wanted to assure you that they, in a very scientific and modern way, had *added* a bunch of stuff. "Oh, goody," your great grandma thought. "They *enriched* it." And she took it home to feed to her chicks, who have somehow managed to live to the age of seventy-five anyway. But before we shake our heads over her gullibility, we have to realize that we are behaving no differently. Marching thoughtlessly counterclockwise doesn't have a whole lot over marching thoughtlessly clockwise.

If an industrial farmer is spraying a pesticide that is a mix of three kinds of cyanide, and it gets to my family's table in doses that would kill an army, I should know more about this than that he is a deacon in his community church, and that his heart is in the right place. That's as may be, but the cyanide is in the wrong place. Flip it around—the same thing goes for the organic farmer. I don't know that what he thinks is good for me *is* in fact good for me, and I need to do more than determine whether his methods are too important to him. I also need to know if his methods are any good.

Now here is the next thing. Once those questions are answered, and we have weeded out the all natural poseurs gooning around in their truck patches, we find that some organic farmers really do know their stuff, and their organic methods really *are* good, and they really do result in a superior product—I get to eat something fresh and healthy, something that didn't spend three months on a truck. But—and this is a point I have made before—that superior product is a luxury that wealthy people get to enjoy. I think they should enjoy it, and I don't have any beef against wealthy people enjoying superior food. I do have a beef against wealthy people pretending they are not wealthy, pretending their luxuries aren't luxuries. I do have a beef against upper middle class NPR listeners strolling down to farmers' markets as though *they* were earthy peasants in touch with the rhythms of the earth. Why are they in touch with the rhythms of the earth? Well, because they are wealthy enough to pay three times more for corn on the cob than a guy who lives in a trailer on the edge of town, works at the sawmill, and buys *his* corn on the cob at Sam's Club, the Philistine.

But Chesterton was no poseur—he was the genuine article, and the contemporary organic foods movement isn't. He wore an artificial and manufactured cape to cover a heart that did nothing but overflow with Christian insight. This, as opposed to those who wear a Central American coarse-woven authenticity cape to cover up the aching hollowness within. There is a difference, as he might say, between a man who stands in the face of all the prevailing winds, and the one who is driven before them. And when we have grasped the difference, we will have also grasped that the difference is not a subtle one.

He had no use for cant and the poseurs who delivered it. The contemporary hipster is a recent phenomenon (in terms of what we used to call in the Navy the uniform-of-the-day), but the broader category of hipster has been with us since at least the time of Rousseau. The type was well-known to Chesterton, and had there been a Whole Foods in Victorian London, we would have had some choice epigrams from him on the kind of poet who shopped for exotic cheeses there. In fact, here's one he did write, long before the word *metrosexual* was even coined: "The old artist remained proud in spite of his unpopularity; the new artist is proud because of his unpopularity; perhaps it is his chief ground for pride."

If you can't find an outlet to plug this into, then you clearly have the wrong kind of adapter.

Chesterton would never, ever cop a pose because he thought it was ironic and clever—although he would grant that he had ordinary human vanity and say that he thought it ironic and clever because he had copped it. He once said that fallacies do not cease to be fallacies simply because they have become fashions, and who better to take this warning to heart than that contemporary class of person for whom virtually *all* intellectual energy is devoted to staying fashionable?

Of course Chesterton loved paradox—he said that a paradox was truth standing on its head to get attention—but he knew the difference between paradox and simple confusion and contradiction. Throughout his body of work, again and again, he demolishes the contradictions of pretension and builds lasting monuments to true Christian irony. One of our current confusions (which Chesterton is not here to address, unfortunately), and which his heirs must therefore take up in their own inadequate fashion, is what to say about a movement whose two patron saints are Wendell Berry and Steve Jobs.

More Chesterton: "Oscar Wilde said that sunsets were not valued because we could not pay for sunsets. But Oscar Wilde was wrong; we can pay for sunsets. We can pay for them by not being Oscar Wilde."

And by not being his descendants.

I live in the Palouse, and I love it here. As we go to print, it is a festival of harvesting gold. While some of my good friends are out there driving their monster industrial machines through the harvest (as they are doing right this minute), they will harvest enough in a brief time to feed a small Third World country through the winter. As they do, I can't think of anything to complain about. It may not result in the highest quality baguette ever, but it is better than starving.

Assume you can get one loaf of bread off one square foot of land, which, estimating conservatively, an American farmer can now do. An acre of ground will get you 43,560 loaves. A six hundred acre farm (a small farm in these parts), will get you 26 million loaves of bread, with another 136,000 loaves thrown in for good measure. I have a hard time thinking of this with any response other than gratitude.

In sum, the Christ-centered aesthetic argument is a good one, as far as it goes. But we need to keep it in its place and recognize it for what it is—a God-given luxury, and a true creational good. But like all creational goods, it frequently finds itself in tension with other creational goods. Quality of food is of course a good. But in a world where starvation exists, so is quantity.

What all this amounts to is that fresh corn tastes better than canned corn, and who knew? So if you want to pay extra for *that*, great. Be our guest. But quit acting like it is a "conscience and responsibility" thing, because canned corn is nutritionally better than no corn.

Unless you are a gourmand with a social conscience and an itch to boss people around.

CHAPTER 6

More on Food Aesthetics

Where do the standards of truth, beauty, and goodness fit into this discussion? If I believe and teach (and I do) that God has given us standards by which to evaluate other areas of our lives, shouldn't I promote standards in the area of food production and preparation?

This is an important question, and it requires descending into autobiography just a tad. I was born in 1953, and grew up, not surprisingly, eating fifties food. I was taught to say grace over all that food, and I am not about to take any of that back now. I am truly and eternally grateful for the casseroles, for the simple fare, for the food I was provided. It was given me by parents who loved me and fed me, and it was given them by a Father who loved us all. God is great, God is good, let us thank Him for our food. We thanked Him for the food, incidentally, and not for food substitutes. Food substitutes would only have resulted in substitute feeding, and if that was what was happening, I would be dead by now.

I was also taught by my parents that we needed to grow up into Christ, and we needed look to Scripture for light and guidance in every aspect of life. We were taught that it is easy for a fish to swim downstream, even if it's dead. Grow up. That desire to grow up into Christ, as the Scriptures invite us to do, has been a central feature of the ministry here. We can do better, without disparaging what was given us before.

But there are two kinds of doing better. One is growing up from good to better (without disparaging the former), and the other is repenting of sin and turning to righteousness (where disparagement is unavoidable). It is essential that we not confuse the two.

I love the gospel songs I grew up on, the kind that we sang at Sunday evening service in the Southern Baptist Church we attended. I find myself singing snatches of them to this day as I walk around town. I don't want to sing them in church—we grew past that. But if I didn't want to sing them in church because I despised them now, then in actual fact, I wouldn't have grown past anything. Rather, that would be regression and falling from my first love. Some songs need to be repented of—for the flippancy, say. But many others need to be loved, honored, and used as a platform to reach higher.

We have very much applied this principle to our food, and to the rituals of our eating. I am not an egalitarian when it comes to food, and I believe that God invites us up into greater and deeper delights. But He doesn't chase us up to higher levels with the whip of guilt. This is a get to, not a got to.

When I was growing up, every evening we would sit down together for the shared family meal. I can't thank God or my parents enough for that. I wouldn't take a hundred billion for it. While my kids were growing up, every evening we would sit down together for the shared family meal. For a number of reasons, all having to do with the grace of God, a culture of feasting has taken root in our church community here, for which we are extremely grateful. And a culture of feasting, incidentally, is not a culture of gorging. Neither is it a culture of snide remarks about people who can only afford to get their milk at Walmart.

Our family still has a sit down meal every evening, and now that we have grandkids, the whole clan sits down every Saturday night for our Sabbath dinner.

On that occasion, we have a toast, we have delighted answers to the Sabbath catechism questions, and we have the best meal of the week—and the meals are great all week. So do I believe in applying aesthetic and reformational principles to our food? Heh. As the apostle Paul might say, I am out of my mind to talk this way, but I have eaten more cheese potatoes than you all. And of course, the real hero in this is Nancy, who puts on the equivalent of a Thanksgiving feast every week.

So, to answer the question above. Yes, I believe in food reformation. Yes, I believe aesthetic principles apply. Yes, I believe we must grow to maturity in this area as in all areas. Christ is Lord. So what am I going on about? What's my deal? It is pretty simple, really. When you have a garden, the first rule is to keep dragons out of it. And pride, snobbery, and false guilt are nothing but three little dragon eggs. That's my deal.

First, aesthetic superiority cannot be achieved simply by laying claim to it. If it were that easy, there would be more famous painters than there are, and more world renowned chefs. Thus far I have kept out of the discussion *what* I believe to be better food, not because I don't have views on the matter, but rather because that is not the central point—at least not at this place in our cultural discussions. We need to master gratitude first, lest we regress. Let us live up to what we have already attained. I would be hard pressed to come up with my favorite verse from the Bible, but one of the contenders would surely be this one:

"And in this mountain shall the Lord of hosts make unto all people a feast of fat things, a feast of wines on the lees, of fat things full of marrow, of wines on the lees well refined" (Isa. 25:6).

I want to be a puritan, not a purist. I want to reformational, not revolutionary. I am a slow food reformer, not a fast food reformer. I am a food catholic, not a food sectarian.

And this brings me to my second point. In any area, the purists are routinely the enemies of any kind of sustained reformation. As Lewis shows in *English Literature in the Sixteenth Century*, it was the high classicists who killed Latin. Sayers makes the same point elsewhere. Over-reaching kills the thing it claims to exalt, right on schedule. If you want the people to listen to (what you deem to be) quality music, 24/7, all you are going to do is create a situation where human nature revolts. You can want musical reformation, as I desperately do, but still recognize that all toney, all the time, is only going to create a backlash, and a right-minded disgust with the attempts to make the soundtrack of your lives into something supplied by National Public Radio. When housewives want to blow through cleaning the kitchen and two bathrooms, what is needed is some Dwight Yoakam, or Fleetwood Mac, or Asleep at the Wheel, turned up to eleven, and not, say, some 17th century music for five recorders, including two of the big ones. It would be terrible to be halfway through the first bathroom and have everybody show up for the wine and cheese party. Not that there is anything wrong with *that*, mind you. Everything in its place.

Purists who insist on their ideal being implemented across the board are their own worst enemies. Everybody needs to get out more. Lighten up. Back to the music example, one of the presents I got for Christmas was the book *1000 Recordings to Hear Before You Die*. I started at the beginning and, thanks to the Internet, have been listening through the whole thing. I have found some great stuff, but there is some pretty weird music out there, let me tell you. When I am done, will I be richer or poorer? Even though one of entries in the A's was ABBA, I will still be the richer. (I should also confess that I stalled out on that project—may get back to it someday.)

In that same spirit, everybody who is into organic food really needs, at least three times a year, to go outside the city limits and have a quarter-pounder at a fast food restaurant. And they need to do it without looking like a rabbi who was just handed a BLT. And they can't call it "cheating," or compromising their principles. Their principles should include it. Budget for it. But fair's fair, and they aren't the only ones who need to stretch themselves. Ecumenism at the table is a healthy exercise, and so I do want to say that I know what escargot, tofu, and art salad taste like. And I didn't used to know. God is great, God is good, let us thank Him for our food. All of it.

"My soul shall be satisfied as with marrow and fatness; and my mouth shall praise thee with joyful lips" (Ps. 63:5)

CHAPTER 7

The Pretense of Omniscience

O kay, what causes what, and how can we know? Let's talk a bit about stewardship, epistemology and food.

One of the central problems in food debates is the conflicting nature of multiple claims made about food. And in order to sort through all of it, we have to address the question of knowledge. In a global economy, how can I know how my food was grown, prepared, processed, packaged, and shipped? Where does simple trust come in? What about gullibility?

Take the example of how animals are treated in food production. "A righteous [man] regardeth the life of his beast: but the tender mercies of the wicked

[are] cruel" (Prov. 12:10). Every Christian should be able to agree on this. If Farmer Smith came into the dining room with meat off the grill, and told us that he had spent four or five satisfying hours that morning torturing the animal we were about to eat, basic decency would prohibit partaking—not to mention one of us punching Smith on the nose. This is because the principle is acknowledged by all, and the facts of the case are not in dispute.

But what do I do if someone tells me I should not have that steak my wife bought at Safeway because his cousin read an article once, he forgets which magazine, that says that cattle are horribly mistreated, and are made to stand in their own filth for year after year. Not only that, but they are injected with evil hormones to make them succulent and tempting to us. And not only *that*, the hormones are supplied to the ranchers free of charge by the CIA as part of their goal to make the American populace more bovine in preparation for the coming coup. How far out there does it have to get before I am allowed to start having some doubts? Or flipped around, how many generations removed from me does "the knowledge" have to get before it ceases to lay any moral claim whatever on me? There are liars, damned liars, and statisticians, as the saying goes.

Now there are plenty of nasty things going on out there in the great wide world that are *true*, and that I don't know about. But this is my point. I am not required by God to modify my behavior on the basis of any pretended omniscience. All attempts to gather a "global view" are variations on the "ye shall be as God" theme. If Paul didn't mind Christians in Corinth getting their pot roast from the local pagan temple, and he *didn't* mind it, then why would he mind if some of my food came from a factory where people were working twelve hour shifts? The earth is the Lord's and the fullness thereof. Don't worry about it.

Narrative accounts about how the world works are *worldview* accounts. Narratival worldview accounts depend on their underlying *religious* assumptions. This applies, across the board, to narrative accounts of how wars begin, how chickens are treated on big chicken farms, how presidents get elected, whether frankenfood will make hair grow on your back, what happens to nutrients when sealed in a can, and so on, down the street and around the corner. When we step out into the world of "how a bill becomes a law," "how a cow becomes a hot dog," and "how Monsanto became the devil," we are stepping into a religiously laden debate. It is not a simple matter of "research" or "science" or "facts." There is no neutrality anywhere. *Everyone* has an agenda, not just the "bad guys."

Back on the farm, if someone accused Farmer Smith of mistreating our dinner, and he said, "I did nothing of the kind," we would be sitting there informally observing Proverbs 18:17. One guy seems really reasonable until you hear the other side, and in our personal, immediate settings it is hard not to hear the other side. Even if we don't understand the basics of justice, the "other side" often *insists* that we hear his case anyway.

On matters of gross injustice in the production of my dinner, I quite agree with the principle. In other words, if I knew a restaurant in town with the best-tasting steak got those fantastic results by flogging its cooks out back, cheating its wholesalers, double-crossing the waitresses on the tips, and sending representatives out to the stockyards every month to taunt the cows, I would not patronize that restaurant. I don't want to bless known scoundrels with my business. So the principle is fine.

But the problem is with that word "known." To assert injustice is not the same thing as proving it. Much ado is made over the concept of "fair trade," for example, but largely by people who don't know what "fair" means, or what "trade" is. In short, I flat

THE PRETENSE OF OMNISCIENCE | 105

don't believe them. Sometimes the business is run by scoundrels, and other times the agitating protesters are the scoundrels. And going back to the first point, how many people who drink fair trade coffee were stampeded into it by a marketing campaign? A lot more skepticism is in order.

The idea of separation is a biblical idea. Come out from among them and be ye holy (2 Cor. 6:17). But in order to do this it is necessary actually to separate on biblical principle and in a biblical way. We need to learn *how* God intends for His people to be distinct. Too often Christians separate from the world in ways that are just one part of the world separating from another part of the world, with Christians tagging along behind for the sake of relevance, but in the name of holiness.

When we participate in the goings-on of a sinful world, does that sin contaminate us? I am not talking about participation in the sin itself, obviously, but in activities that are connected to sinful activity, or which had their origins in sinful activity. May I live in those portions of North America that were stolen from the Indians? May I drive on highways that go over property that were seized unjustly by eminent domain? May I buy an automobile when the carburetor was manufactured by slave labor in mainland

China? How about the carburetor and the distributor cap? May I buy gasoline from a joint that has three racks of porn behind the counter? May I buy books from a company that has a soft porn division? May I buy mutual funds that include corporate farms and plantations in the portfolio?

Now the issue is not whether Christians are called to be salt and light, and it is not whether we are supposed to have a salutary influence in this world. Of course we are. The question is rather how this is to be done. The question concerns God's mechanism for this. What does He tell us to do, and what does He tell us not to worry about?

So there are two basic principles here. One is that when the Bible does address the question of financial separation from those who do not honor God, it goes in exactly the opposite direction that our instincts tell us to. We say that it would contaminate us if we "subsidized" the evil company, but the Bible tells us not to worry about it. Does buying meat from the shambles in Corinth (1 Cor. 10:25) help provide an income stream for the idolatrous temple services? Sure it does, but who is worried about it? Not God! God has other ways of affecting their income stream (Acts 19:24–27). Buy their meat, but not their silver figurines. That will be quite enough to get their attention.

The earth is the Lord's and the fullness thereof. This is a bedrock principle. The sooner Christians act on the basis of it, the sooner we will persuade the pagans that it is the truth of God. How can we get them to abandon their view that "this territory is the devil's" *when we share that view with them?* How can we tell them to abandon their fragmented view of the world when we have a fragmented view of the world?

Now if this is the case when the sin is on this end of the economic transaction—you can see the porn behind the counter, you can see the smoke from the sacrificial fires a block away from the place where you buy the meat—then how much more would it apply when the sin is on the other side of the world, and you only heard about it through a series of supposes, hear-say conservations, and a Michael Moore confusion-montage.

So the second principle is this one. Accusations of wrongdoing on the other side of the world are not the same thing as establishing the truth of the accusation from the mouths of two or three witnesses, with cross-examination and *diligent inquiry that presupposes the innocence of the accused.*

Suppose someone was talking about how evil a particular corporation was, and how necessary it was for us to do our Christian duty and never buy any of their product lines again. I would say that this is clearly insufficient. This charge, if true, means that we need to round up the board of trustees for this corporation, line them up against the nearest stucco wall, hand them each a blindfold, and shoot them all. This kind of evil must be dealt with. But suppose, when we start to talk this way, the fellow urging us to boycott the evil company starts backpedaling. Why would he do that? Because to shoot anybody, even a board of trustees, it is necessary to actually prove your allegations. But in order to get Christians to feel guilty about the scarves, oranges, coffee, and hand-bags that they buy . . . well, it turns out that it is not necessary to prove anything at all.

In *God in the Dock*, Lewis addresses in his typical trenchant way the dangers of national repentance. And, of course, one of the first things to note is that there is absolutely nothing wrong with national re-pentance, the real kind. But sinners have a consistent way of foisting the guilt of their moral failings off onto the backs of the nearest available abstraction—the age, the nation, the corporations, or the trends.

But the fundamental moral duties in Scripture are individual. "Thou" is not a peculiar kind of holy-speak found in sacred texts, but is simply the seventeenth century singular. "Thou shalt not" means "You, yeah, you there in the third row, shalt not . . ." It is this kind of thing that used to make people squirm during sermons, but not so much anymore.

I am an active participant in my food chain, and I occupy a particular place in it. My moral duties are strongest right next to me, and they are weakest (to the extent that they exist at all) at the far side of the food chain.

This is not to say that moral responsibility cannot be transmitted along the food chain. Surely it can, as when my buddy shoplifts something from Safeway so we can share it for dinner. Eating stolen goods that I watched get stolen is morally problematic, and I cheerfully grant it. But I am here talking about my supposed complicity in the strange oaths that the foreman in the Texas pecan orchard swore at his underpaid migrant workers, in the season before those pecans from said ranch made their way through thirteen other morally problematic checkpoints on their way to my pie.

Now the reason it is wrong to invert everything like this is that obsessing about distant sin far, far away is almost always for the purpose of making room for sin near at hand (the personal kinds of sins that people commit against other people), or to atone for that same kind of personal guilt. It is either trying to get rid of guilt or make room for it, or both.

The bizarre moral duty to assume responsibility for corporations on the other side of the world that might be doing something wrong is a moral duty that has been brought center stage and foisted upon us by a drunken, stoned, fornicating, sodomizing, porn-watching, unborn child-murdering generation. And so what happens when blind men lead? The Lord spoke of the phenomenon once. And speaking of finicky diets, these are the people who strain at gnats and eat the camel. And to make it perfectly plain, swallowing unclean camels is a dietary issue.

If all this were happening in an era when obedience to the Ten Commandments had broken out all over, and we were all looking around with a culture-wide Westminster Larger Catechism gleam in our eye, looking to find the next level we could kick it up to, so that we could all become the Navy Seals of responsible biblical casuistry, I confess that such a circumstance would make it necessary to take it all more seriously (than I am currently doing). But we don't live in that generation. We live in a time when all of the Ten Commandments are broken routinely, and half of them are mocked openly. And this is the generation that wants to lecture me about eating a chicken that Old MacDonald never sang E-I-E-I-O to. Wisdom is vindicated by her children. We piped but ye did not dance. We bought the Happy Meal but ye did not play with the toy.

On top of that, those quadrants of the church that are most likely to share in these various guilt-spasms—most likely to wallow in guilt over somebody else's corporate malfeasance, most likely to urge us to flush only when we absolutely have to, most likely to learn the stewardship requirements of Genesis from *The New York Times*—are the same quadrants of the church ordaining homos and all the rest of it. Thought experiment. If I were to write a breathtakingly honest book review about the brutally honest transexual journey that one former fundamentalist had to take, as he made his way from condemnation to the liberation of self-acceptance, what kind of theological rag would publish it? What kind of publication wouldn't? And which of the two would be most likely to publish some stewardship screed or other, arguing that responsible Christians have a moral obligation to protect the planet in just the ways that the lead singer of your favorite alternative rock band would approve of? Right. Thought so. So let's stop pretending that we don't know where the pressures are coming from.

As Christians discuss the morality of their food choices, one of the most compelling arguments for opting out of the chicken-sandwich-at-Arby's lifestyle is that brought by those who maintain that large-scale factory farming is necessarily abusive to the animals involved. I want to state two guiding principles now which inform my thinking on that issue.

The first is that, if we grant the abuse, the objection is more than sound—it is compelling (Prov. 12:10). It is false to say that men do not owe anything to their animals. We clearly do not owe the *same* thing to animals that we owe to one another, because a Christian man can treat an animal decently that he winds up having for dinner. But nevertheless, *mutatis mutandis*, we clearly owe our animals respect, and this applies both to the twenty chickens in the barnyard, and to the twenty thousand chickens in that large building on the horizon over there. That is the first principle.

But the second principle has to be remembered as well. Animals are not the same as humans, for we bear the image of God and they do not. But animals are *similar* to humans; we can empathize with them to varying degrees, and, depending on the circumstances, we should. But this similarity leads to the second point. Just as we all should know intuitively that abuse is wrong, so we should also all know intuitively that abuse is counterproductive. At some point pretty soon in the process, a significantly abusive chicken rancher would run into the law of diminishing returns, and the results would spell disaster for *him*.

Back to Farmer Smith, if he were in the habit of tormenting his cows all day long at close intervals, would his milk production go up or down? This is not a trick question. Animals do not perform well under abusive pressure, any more than humans do. We are similar that way. But in 1935, it took 16 weeks to get chickens up to a scrawny 2.8 pounds. In 2006, it took 7 weeks to get them up to 6 pounds. To argue that these results were achieved by making their chicken lives hellish is, at some significant level, counterintuitive.

But if the argument then shifts, and it is maintained that this is all done with hormones and mirrors, and that the chickens are living the luxurious life of the doomed, and that the hormones are bad for you and your sandwich, then we should at least notice that the abuse argument has been dropped. We are no longer talking about chickens in torment, and are now talking about how the splendid condition of the chickens was achieved by cheating. There are reasonable questions to raise there, I am sure, but they are not the same questions that Proverbs 12:10 creates.

If someone at the gym, during your morning workout, tells you in passing that "studies have shown" that "big corporations" are using "an ingredient found in rat poison" in their most popular breakfast cereals, what do you know? You know precisely what you knew before, which is nothing. But you might feel like you know something, and you might pass it on. And when the telephone-game word gets to someone who digs in his heels and says, "I don't know how that could be true," and that person is treated as though he is being culpably and willfully ignorant, in the same class with the fellow who refuses to look out the back window to see what Farmer Smith is doing to that poor critter, then we have gotten to the point where one person is being clobbered by another person's hidden religious dogmatism. The *clobbering* is not hidden; the religious *faith* assumptions are. The *imperialism* is the giveaway, not the position itself. A food nut might tell me something that happens to be quite true. But that doesn't mean everything is balanced. If someone is thinking about food in the wrong way, letting food get into his evangel, it is not surprising that an ardent and zealous "evangelism" results. But we should actually be able to go for years without worrying what our friends had for lunch today. None of our business, as the apostle Paul might say if he were here. I don't worry about whether my friends got their teeth brushed this morning either.

But it is the mark of certain kind of dogmatic mind that the farther away from the evidence he gets, the more certain he gets. For him this is a simple way to resolve the problems of "food knowledge"—the old, reliable mechanism of mere dogmatism. Assert, assert, and assert some more. But no matter how many times you tell me, I still don't know. Not only that, I could read a stack of books that hew the party line and still not know. I can watch thirteen muckraking documentaries on factory foods in a row, and still not know. The truth about global food production has— oh, just estimating now—about fifteen thousand significant variables in it. If I dropped everything right now to begin researching where the chicken sandwich I had for lunch came from, after about ten years I *might* be getting close. And judging from the behavior of a lot of true believers on the pressing subject of my lunch, I also might be a lot farther away than when I started.

I am not saying this as a nihilistic relativist. I know plenty of things. My doctrine of original sin tells me that if a government provides subsidies to do rotten things, there will probably be some takers. I know *that*. What I don't know is whether Company A took such subsidies from Government B with the perfidious intent of killing off Consumer C, that is, me.

Maybe Competitor D is paying Propagandist E to tell me lies about Company A and Government B so that they will be in a better position to sell me stuff because they want me dead the organic way. The pharmaceuticals are "big business," eh? Like alternative suppliers *aren't*? Kraft "packages and sells" their products in a way that commodifies unnaturally. Oh, and the Hippie Mama Free-Range Macaroni *isn't* packaged and sold? Look around yourself, use common sense, and apply that common sense to *everyone* in the debate. Take it easy, make your own decisions, and avoid every form of food imperialism.

Prudence and wisdom are good. If a bunch of my friends are in the hospital with salmonella they got at a local bistro, should this affect my behavior? Wal, shore. That is simple prudence, commended to us in the book of Proverbs. But nameless fears and ungrounded guilt are bad, evil, from the devil, straight out of the pit. A lot of the people who traffic in food phobias could have benefited greatly from an eighth grade logic course. If you tell me that something I am putting into my mouth is going to kill me, you have my attention. But if you waste that opportunity by going on to completely redefine words like "toxic," "poison," and "kill," you have lost my attention again. I have better things to do than try to calculate how many weeks one slice of cinnamon toast is going to take off my life.

A man and his wife were both unfortunately killed in a car accident, and floated up to the pearly gates, as those gates appear in countless cartoons and jokes. St. Peter was giving them the tour, and he showed them their mansion, and the ultimate golf course right next to it, and the celestial country club on the other side, and the buffet at that club was beyond all description. There were mounds and heaps of *every* kind of delicacy. The wife asked what everything cost, and they were told that this was heaven, and that everything was free. As they continued to take it all in, the husband was getting more and more agitated, upset, worked up, gloomy, and eventually downright sullen. Finally, St. Peter could ignore it no longer and asked, "Is anything wrong, sir?" With that the husband wheeled on his wife—"If it hadn't been for you and those *bran* muffins, I would have been here ten years ago!"

Some may wonder why I appear to be on a food jag. The principle is a simple one. If, for example, I encounter two or three instances of husbands getting angry with their wives and families, you can bet that I will assume that these three guys do not represent an exhaustive list, and the problem is going to start showing up in my sermons and in things I write. A preacher's job is, in part, to attack sin. In the same way, when I encounter food issues of various kinds that are stumbling Christians, sometimes grievously, it has to be addressed. Secondly, when certain memes start to circulate in the Christian community and those memes are biblically false, then it is necessary to correct them. Those memes don't stumble everybody, but they do stumble some very sad cases. So the standard always has to be the straight edge of the Word.

That said, here are some basic biblical principles. The starting point is that God doesn't care what you eat. A man is not defiled by what goes into his mouth, but rather by what comes out of it (Mark 7:18,23). Food for the stomach, and the stomach for food, but God will destroy them both (1 Cor. 6:13). Eat what is set before you (Luke 10:8). Max nix, everybody. But just because God doesn't care what you eat—tofu, bean sprouts, Wonder bread, red meat, peanut butter and brown sugar sandwiches, He just doesn't care—it does not follow from this that food is a sin-free zone. People sin all the time with their food, just not in their food. They can do this through gluttony, poor stewardship of their bodies, self-righteous censoriousness, bringing their own special food to someone's house when they were invited for dinner, laziness, food snobbery, and more. But these are all motive issues, heart issues. We sin with food all the time, and God still doesn't care what we eat. Mastering that distinction is crucial.

In the same way, it is certainly possible to sin in the production of food. People do that all the time too, and mark me down as one preacher who thinks they should quit it. If I had a dairy farmer as a member of the church who tormented his animals, that is the kind of thing that could end with an excommunication (Prov. 12:10). If you lived next door and knew for a fact that he was an evil man who had it in for cows—besides thinking he was in the wrong line of work—you would also be well within your rights to avoid doing business with him. But if the public rhetoric about all this has gotten to the point where you think a rancher is abusing his cattle simply because he is feeding them corn, and you want other Christians to recoil in horror along with you, as though his feedlot were an abortion mill, it is long past time to walk it back.

So here is my proposal for common ground. The lordship of Christ extends to everything, food consumption and food production included. Whatever we do, whatever we eat or drink, we should do it all to the glory of God (1 Cor. 10:31). But in order to glorify

God in this, we have to take our standards straight from the Bible, and there is plenty of teaching on it. We must never take our standards from the arbiters of cool, what the apostle John called "the world."

Just as we can't know everything about food chain ethics, we can't know everything about the "healthiness" of food, but we often make a pretense of omniscience on that front, as well.

Back in the 1920s, everybody knew that *fillintheblank* was bad for you. In the 1950s, they knew the opposite thing, that something else was good for you, say, *fillinanotherblank*. In some instances, we still think the same thing as they did, and in others we think something completely different. Gone are the days when a particular brand of cigarette could be marketed as a "choice of doctors," but equally gone are the times when we knew that processing grains made more nutrition available to the eater. Whole grains are a great delivery module for getting nutritional value down to the sewer treatment plant.

But there is a difference between believing in progress, which I generally do, and believing that it is automatic, and therefore necessarily favors whatever we are all thinking now. This latter approach is not a thoughtful position, but is rather a form of generational egocentricity. It doesn't take much effort to believe that your beliefs are correct (Prov. 16:2). That is what makes them your beliefs, after all. What takes a lot of wisdom is to budget for the *possibility* that you are not correct.

Since human nature has not changed since the '20s, or the '50s, when do you think it will occur to us that we are doing the same kind of thing that they used to do, assuming certain things to be true with a knowing chuckle, and simply because we read about it in *Reader's Digest*? They had their "what everybody knows," and we have ours. Theirs are easy for us to see, and the knowing chuckle arises unbidden. Ours are impossible for us to see. They are impossible to hear about also, because whenever someone tries to point something out, they are drowned out by the shrieks.

You ask for an example?

Well, okay, if you promise not to freak out. Obesity does not represent a major health crisis in America today. How's that?

Let me simply note that the American people have a deep faith in certain things that actual science cannot touch. We can measure this faith by looking at the areas in which our politicians and regulators are allowed to hassle us, and the areas where we will not allow them to speak reassurance to us. Because we are a technocratic society, we pretend that this is a matter of science when it is nothing of the kind.

This is what I mean. Do we have ample scientific reasons for believing that drinking alcohol in moderation provides positive health benefits? We most certainly do. Now, the question is this. Can you imagine merchants of these health-giving benefits being allowed to put the results of these studies on the label? Not without a fight. If there is anything negative, that could go on there. The surgeon general has seen to it that we are all warned about possible risks to pregnant women, operators of cars or machinery, and we are informed that the contents of the bottle "may cause health problems." Now how many health benefits would have to be shown by how many scientific studies before a brewery or vintner would be allowed to say so? On the label, or in an ad? Well, the answer is that until we repent of certain underlying assumptions about God's grouchiness, the number of scientific studies is irrelevant. We think we already know, but we don't. We have defined fish as anything larger than the mesh on our net, and what our net don't catch ain't fish.

Here is another example, a little closer to home. The laughable BMI manner of calculating whether someone is overweight gives us a "scientific" basis for joking learnedly about a friend's breakfast order at a restaurant being a "heart attack on a plate." The problem is that America has an anorexic eye, and we are blind to the fact that our health problems are not caused by butter. Someone who is fifty pounds overweight is far less likely to have health problems than someone who is five pounds underweight. Is this valuable information going to show up any time soon on the side of your biscuit box?

Morbid obesity is a problem, followed closely by the problems of being skinny. Skinny is not healthy. Those cute girls in the J. Crew catalog are going to die next week. Yo-yo dieting is a health problem, that's true enough. But being a bit overweight is a health benefit. Hold on, I have to type a bit faster before they come and take me away . . .

In order to sell something to people you have to create a demand for it. In order to sell billions of dollars of something to people, you have to create a *huge* demand for it. This has now been successfully done— with pills, with weight loss programs, with healthy food regimes, and with more pills.

We live in a time when the government assumes way too much regulatory responsibility for food and drugs, and we should recognize that this does not eliminate the idea of a free market price. It just moves the free market price from the food and drugs, where it ought to be, and creates a free market price for regulators, where it ought not to be. Anybody who thinks that you can give the FDA complete control over what you can put in your mouth, and not set up a bidding war in the food industry as a consequence, is a person who probably has a very sunny disposition, and who is routinely surprised at what people do to him. Every morning is a new day.

So my request is this. Simply allow for the *possibility* that our generation is a herd, just like the others, and stampedes, just like the others. Budget for the possibility that when you go to a restaurant, and you look over their "heart healthy" choices, that they are nothing of the kind. Just acknowledge that it's *possible*. Maybe it is very tasty, and if so, be my guest. Whether that entrée is tasty can be ascertained without twenty more years of scientific research. So just allow for the likelihood that in certain areas our generation is just as dumb as all the others.

I am going to wax a bit autobiographical, and I hope that's all right with everybody. This is not so that I can talk about me, but rather because I can't talk about how I figure things without talking about I how figure things.

When it comes to matters of health, God has been extraordinarily kind to me despite a dearth of bran muffins. I have been preaching for the same congregation for thirty-nine years, and haven't once been out of the pulpit because of sickness. For that same stretch of time and a bit longer, I have been confined to bed once—a case of the flu—and that was for one day. I don't take any of this for granted, and I thank God for His mercy to me in it.

And let me hasten to add something else—I know that saying *anything* like this while doing a touchdown dance is just asking for a heart attack tomorrow, and so I am refraining entirely from the touchdown dance part. This is all grace from God and so I am not saying this as a boast. But I *am* using it as a premise in an argument. If I have been making myself deadly sick for all these years, shouldn't I be sick by now? Does anyone see why I am dubious when I am confidently told by someone that my food is making me feel terrible when I feel great? I don't *deserve* to feel great, but that does not change the fact that I *do*.

Now I am aware that someone could come back at me and say that it doesn't matter that I am eating all this poison because I obviously have the constitution and character of Rasputin, and that's not a *good* thing, he hastens to add. Well, okay, but shouldn't it also be reasonable to think that I might not take up this line of argument myself?

At the same time, over the years, some of the sickliest people I know are people who have positively hovered over their diets. I know that correlation is *not* causation, and that there are a number of ways this could go. There are people who do this on doctor's orders, there are people who do this because doctors can't help them and they are desperate, there are people who do this because get religious reassurance and comfort through what they put in their mouths, there are people who do this because all their friends are doing it, there are people who do this because they read an article, there are people who do this because they have a deep gnostic loathing of their bodies, and there are people who convince themselves that they must be sick and then proceed to make themselves really sick through a self-treatment regimen that centers on eating a lot of something I wouldn't touch with a barge pole. I am *not* saying that everyone who differs with me on this topic is in this last category—not even close, please note—but I can say that as a pastor I *have* dealt with a fair number of people in this last category—people who have done serious damage to their careers, their bodies, and their marriages. Put another way, I am not at all convinced that "heath food" is healthy in any exceptional way, and I *am* convinced that too much emphasis on it, just like too much emphasis on regular food, is unhealthy.

Cigarettes got their name *coffin nails* long before the surgeon-general did his thing. This is because people have eyes in their heads. We can do the same thing with food. Be reasonable and moderate, and use your head. But just as we can't know everything about food chain ethics, we can't know everything about the "healthiness" of food, and our hubristic pretense of omniscience in both cases betrays our idolatry not only of food, but of self.

To be responsible, we don't have wait from some ultimate decree from Science on High, or, to use the pattern of what we usually do, treat the latest decree of Science on High as though it *were* the ultimate decree. Butter, bad, margarine, good. No, wait . . . cholesterol, bad. No, wait, except for the good kind of cholesterol. Fiber good for heading off colon cancer. No, wait . . . guess not. And the one thing you must not do in this topsy-turvy world of constant transition is act like you remember what we were all avoiding like crazy this time last year.

I am not saying this to disparage medical research on what is good for us—I *like* the fact that scientists are willing to correct themselves and change. And when they do, I think that we, generally, for the most part, should go along—as we feel like it. We need to hold these things gratefully . . . and loosely. The thing we have *stop* doing is treating these provisional judgments as though they were an infallible dogma from the Baltimore Catechism. And that is a standard we should have no trouble with . . . provided we stay full of gratitude and common sense, and free from fear.

Someone might tell me that if I don't stop grilling carcinogens into my meat, then I will *die*. And so my question would be, "If I stop, and do everything you say, what will I die of then?"

Another question concerns basic health issues. I would take the same general approach here. That is, I would grant the principle, but dispute the plethora of contemporary applications. If we concentrate on the *how* and *why* we eat together, and the emphasis is on love, of course a faithful mom is going to make sure her kids get enough citrus to enable them to avoid scurvy. That is all to the good, and is common sense. To my detractors, I would simply say this: I approve of little children not getting scurvy.

The problem here is not what we know, but rather what we *think* we know—and how quickly we start pressuring and condemning others on the basis of what we think we know. The issue here is that claims about health and well-being are very much like claims about global economics. A lot of what is said just ain't so. Daniel was willing to put his dietary request to the chamberlain to the test. After ten days, are we ruddier or are they ruddier? After ten days are we fairer and fatter in flesh, or are they (Dan. 1:14–16)? Mom, have your husband run a blind taste test for you—put an organic apple and a regular Safeway apple in the kids' lunches for ten days, without telling you which one is getting which one. Then after ten days, you tell him which kid has been eating healthier.

But if the claims stand up, as they do with Vitamin C and scurvy, then the point stands. Sure. Everything else being equal, a family should be served a healthy, well-balanced meal. Mom should not let her teen-aged son ruin his dinner by wolfing a bag of chips half an hour before. Marshmallow pop tarts are not the breakfast of champions. My phight against phood pharisaism should not be taken as a ringing endorsement of maple bars with bacon on them . . . although I might try one sometime. It is simply that a lot of the dietary harum-scarum these days is based on statistical hoodoo, galloping fads, shrewd marketing, and crony capitalism (again, see the first point). Again, a bit more skepticism before making any claims about food that reflect on any person's standing with God.

And if the reader takes one thing away from this book, I would hope that this would be it—we are not put right with God or kept right with God by means of what we choose to eat or not eat. The kingdom of God is not a matter of eating and drinking, but of righteousness, peace, and joy in the Holy Spirit (Rom. 14:17).

You don't need to be so skeptical that you won't try anything new. You can sell the food options without selling the guilt. In fact, the pastor said, that is what you *must* do.

CHAPTER 8

The Pretense of Omnipotence

F ood, Inc., is a 2008 movie about the unsavory side of the food manufacturing industry in America.[6] Before I level a few criticisms at it (only a few—no need to answer every twig and leaf when the trunk is right there) I want to mention a few credit where credit is due moments. The makers of this movie were foodists, but did not appear to be insane foodists. This enabled *them* to give credit where credit is due. Twenty bushels per acre used to be really rocking, and now we get 200. A century ago, a farmer used to be able to feed six to eight people, and now it is around 126. And there is one visual shot of a small

6 *Food, Inc.,* DVD, directed by Robert Kenner (Dallas: Magnolia Pictures, 2008).

mountain of corn that would make any ordinary person want to stand up and salute. Looked like Joseph was getting ready for hard times in Egypt.

Nevertheless, the movie was still a propaganda piece, competently assembled, which means that it was an embodiment of the need for understanding Proverbs 18:17, now more than ever. There were all sorts of moments where you found yourself thinking, "Interesting. Wonder why they would do that?" But we never find out. Defenders of the film could say here that multiple times we saw something like the phrase "representatives of fill-in-the-blank company declined to appear in this film." But of course, when you consider how those who *did* appear were represented, it would seem that the no-shows had a better grasp of what was going on.

But that is all we need say about that kind of thing. Like Aunt Dahlia's cook, Anatole, I can take a few smooths with the rough. The central problem with the movie is that it was a movie made by idolatrous statists for idolatrous statists, with the main antagonists being more idolatrous statists. It is hard to make a battle between two different kinds of crony capitalists into a battle between light and darkness, but they labored hard (and unsuccessfully) to do it. For Christians to think of this movie as anything other than a significant part of the problem is to reveal real deficiencies in how biblical worldview thinking is currently understood.

Every real problem identified in the movie—for there were some substantial ones, along with the pretend ones—was a problem created by overweening government interference in the market. And a number of times, this government interference was created by the hue and cry of reformers from a previous generation, who were demanding that those in authority "do something." And is this not the very definition of the modern reformer—someone who identifies a problem and wants "something done"—*whether or not it makes things better or worse*?

Over and over again, the movie pointed out how the savior of government had failed in its saving duties, and then the call of the movie was for government to rise up and save us. We need an Elijah to tell them to cry out louder. You cut yourselves with knives while you dance around the altar—maybe you need a sharper knife? Bigger knife? Turn the music up?

Here are some real problems with our industrial food manufacturing system—all of which were illustrated and shown in some fashion by this movie. These are problems that do to justice what the meat-packing plants do to cows. A short list: unjust agricultural

134 | CONFESSIONS OF A FOOD CATHOLIC

subsidies, unjust immigration law, unjust patent law, the gross injustices of tort law, and the unjust revolving door that enables industry lobbyists to become government regulators of those same industries— anybody picking up a pattern here? What is the common denominator? C'mon, this is not a trick question. You got it—the iniquity and/or incompetence of the state in such affairs. And what do the makers of the movie want? More power given to the state! We need another regulation. Somebody pass a law. Get that legislation through. But to call for regulation of industry is to call for just this kind of crony capitalism, what I have elsewhere called crapitalism. *This is what regulation does*. This is hair of the dog that bit you reform, which is to say, no reform at all, no solution at all. Not content with faux omniscience, the state has made a grab at omnipotence, as well. But the solution to idolatry is not more idolatry.

Without going into it in great detail, let me give a brief overview of how it should work, lest I be written off as a libertarian naysayer. I am no anarchist. But neither do I think that the state is the Almighty God, in whom we are to live and move and have our being. The government has no business *regulating* this kind of thing. But they do have the solemn responsibility to *define*, in a weights and measures sense. The king is not overstepping his bounds if he defines a shekel, a cubit, a Troy ounce of gold, or a pound of ground beef. Define it, and then outlaw lying, stealing, and cheating. That would solve the real problems identified by this movie. And as for the many imaginary ones, we would be enabled to go back to minding our own business and thanking God for His abundant provision.

From time to time the authorities haul in some renegade cheese maker, and those who love bureaucratized food safety all breathe a sigh of relief. This kind of tyranny is heavy-handed enough to get noticed by those who yearn for food freedom—as I do—but not so noticed generally that we can get the food fascists to stop it. Yet.

There are two basic points that need to be made about this. The first is that the government does have a role in food safety—but it is not the role of preventative regulation. Rather, in a realm of food libertarianism, the government would set the definitions and standards. This is what a fluid ounce is, and that is what counts as cleaning a chicken.

These standards would not be enforced by food inspectors before the fact, but would rather be used whenever an action had been brought by a dissatisfied or food-poisoned customer. The civil magistrate would publish, before the fact, what weights and measures they are going to use to adjudicate legal actions and disputes. An action could be brought either against Tyson or Ma Beedle's Chicken Ranch.

Once the contaminated food were traced back to the offending source, if it were shown that the problem had been caused because Ma Beedle or Tyson had different views (than reasonable people do) on what cleaning a chicken meant, then the assigned damages would be more severe. But the food producer would be liable for the costs associated with the problem, even if the contamination slipped through generally reasonable processes.

When it come to matters of food safety, anybody who has had a batch of bad oysters can attest to the fact that we need a referee to sort things out after the fact. Feelings can run high.

The second big issue has to do with where the real threats to food freedom are actually coming from. Before saying what follows I do want to note that I believe alternative food producers should be free to sell their unpasteurized milk off the back of their pick-up truck if they want to. We are all Christians here, and we all have to go to Heaven sometime. I believe that in a free society, we should all be allowed to take our own risks.

The price of this risk taking is that there must be no whining when the price of that risk comes due—whether for the customer, who got what he paid for, or for the proprietor of the small family farm who will be put out of business by one bad batch of milk. The guys who drive their milk around the country in eighteen wheelers will not be put under by one bad batch, and this is part of the cost of freedom. Freedom can be harder on those who don't have as much money. But it is still worth it for all of us.

What we cannot have is a system that regulates the "big guy" and then leaves the little guy alone. Once establish regulations before the fact, then the big guys will get control of the regulators. "Regulations" to "reform everything" is how we get crony capitalism. This means if you want freedom for the little guy you have to have it for the big guy.

And this relates to one other observation about food freedom. For every small alternative dairyman being oppressed by an overweening state, there are a thousand conventional merchants being oppressed. Food freedom means food freedom. This should include, on a equal footing, the guy who wants to sell you his curds and whey right out of the cow almost, and the guy who wants to sell you 16 ounces of sody pop.

In doing this, we have to distinguish levels of intrusiveness and bossiness, represented by the conventional approach to food safety, and the new foodie approach. As should be plain from what I have written above, I do have foundational disagreements with our current approach to food safety, and want to see it completely reformed. The old system was the set up for the new tyrants. But I still want to make a distinction. In the old days, health inspectors would drop in on restaurants in order to enforce basic hygiene, and to prevent any of the customers from departing this world in paroxysms of pain later that same week. There was a fairly straight line connection between what they were seeking to discourage and what they were trying to prevent—a line that just lasted for just hours.

The new cries for regulation coming from what might be called the foodie left are being done in the name of health and safety (just like the old days), but they are not trying to prevent agonizing deaths later this week. Rather, they are trying to usher in a food utopia, by means of regulations and taxes. They have a vision for the good life and, by George, you had better come along. They want it mandated that your apple will have been locally grown, which has nothing to do with dying a slow death as far as I can see.

The foodie left are totalitarians of the plate. All the frenzies that they get going, whether it is about sugar, or gluten, or locally produced food, and so forth, are frenzies that serve the same function that the global warming frenzy tried to produce—more state power, *exhaustive* state power.

If you like to eat what you like to eat, this means that you are a human being. If you are morally indignant about the food choices of others, this means you are well on the way to becoming a food leftist.

Leftism is that impulse that wants to establish coercion and call it community. Apply the coercive impulse to food and farming choices, and you have the food leftist.

And it begins with the indignation. Once the indignation is established, it becomes possible to draw on a hidden premise that too many Americans share— that sins should be crimes—and move from that position to the idea that made-up sins should be made into real crimes.

When the food regulators change their minds, and start cracking down on *this* product instead of *that* product, this is simply part of the way authoritarian regimes operate. In a despotism, sometimes this is in favor and sometimes that—it can be an official, or a policy, or a method of manufacturing cheese—but regardless, the right of the despotism to continue being a despotism is always in favor. *That* doesn't change.

This obviously does not mean that it is impossible to sin with food. Food leftists are sinning with other people's food. And you can always go old school and sin with your own food. If your approach is all-four-feet-in-the-trough, then perhaps you are a piggy-piggy glutton. If you have a couple bottles of whiskey in your cubicle at work, then maybe you are not the suave 1950's advertising executive you think you are. Maybe you are just an aspiring drunk. And if you are a fastidious eater, and cannot be troubled to be a charitable guest at the table of another, then you are an enemy of love.

In the meantime, every Christian who understands the gospel must fight—as part of our sanctification—the impulse to despise the food that God has given to somebody else. This applies even if the apple was not locally grown, if the coffee was not certified fair trade, if the bread came from a monoculture crop, if the asparagus was modified to taste horrible to asparagus predators, or if the food in question has "chemicals" in it.

We live in a sinful and fallen world, so food must indeed be sanctified. But the only thing that sanctifies it is the gravy of grace and gratitude (1 Tim. 4:4–5).

These numbers are approximations for the most part, sketched out on the back of a napkin. They may be a reflection of my deficient education in math growing up, or of me believing the wrong web site on how much hay an acre of grassland produces, or perhaps a function of some other gross personal deficiency of mine. However, these should give us some idea of what sustainability might mean.

Idaho is a big state, 83,574 square miles to be exact. With 640 acres per square mile, this gives us 53,487,360 acres. Let's keep this simple, round up, and call it 54 million. Let us assume that it is pure grassland.

It takes about 20 acres to provide enough hay to feed a 1,200-pound cow for a year. Let's slaughter the cows at a year old, and assume we can get 600 pounds of usable meat from that cow. That one cow will provide 9,600 ounces of beef, which translates to 1,600 six-ounce portions. That would, rounding up, feed five people for a year, with each one getting a six-ounce portion a day. So, then, twenty acres will provide a family of five a daily portion of meat for a year.

That means our Idaho meadow could do the same for 2.7 million families of five, or 13.5 million people. There are just shy of 7 billion people in the world. If we divide that number by our 13.5 million, we discover how many meadowlike Idahos it will take to keep us in business. It would take 519 of them. And that is just for the beef.

Since North America would take up 113 of these Idahos, that means that four and a half North

Americas, were they nothing but grassland for grass-fed cattle, could feed the world for a year.

Keep in mind that these 7 billion people for the most part could not live on the land that is producing their beef, so they would (for the most part) have to live on the one and a half North Americas left of the world's available land, trying to figure out how to get themselves some chicken for change, and maybe a veggie or two. So the entire population of the world would need to move to that one spot.

And now let's talk about sustainability again.

But before talking about sustainability at the level of food and food production, we should first consider the sustainability of ideas.

One thing that is not really sustainable is fear mongering. That is why faddists are nomadic. They stay camping on one fear fad until their cattle have grazed it out, and then they move on to the next one. In the 19th century, for example, there was this thing called Fletcherism—the practice of learning how to masticate your food, and I mean mashticate it. Overweight people often bolt their food, and we shouldn't do that, and besides the reason God gave us thirty-two teeth was because each bite needs to be chewed at least thirty-two times. Sounds like something you could learn on the Internet, but they didn't have that back then, so we are left wondering where it came from. Everybody is all about it for a while, but then something happens, like facts coming out, and rather than stay and deal with the facts, it is time for those who love their gypsy ways to move on.

In the nomadic lifestyle, the location is not sustainable, although the practice of moving from place to place can be carried on (at least by some) for quite a while. Part of the trick is to be able to get the true believers to not remember that you are trying to get them to drop the very thing that they picked up ten years ago because you demanded it. Butter, no, margarine, no, no margarine, butter again! The chicken skin is fatty, fatty, fatty, and what are you eating all that industrial skinless chicken for, you doof? Split wood, not atoms, but turns out that wood fires make lots of smoke. The coming ice age is coming, the globe is warming, and the science is settled, no, wait. Turns out the globe got so hot it cooked the books.

This is not about food directly, but allow me to make a prediction here, because it illustrates this mindset wonderfully. Right now, wind power is sexy and cool, and every visual image of the modern wind generators is propaganda designed to make you think majestic and sustainable thoughts. Kind of like the British Israelites who thought the smoke stacks of the Industrial Revolution were belching forth the Shekinah glory. But anybody who drives down the Columbia basin with eyes open should be able to tell you what a blot on the landscape they are (an impressive blot, but a blot nonetheless). However, currently it is a most cool blot. But here's my prediction—that impression will turn within ten years or so, and wind generators all over tarnation will become a silent and perfidious testimony of the avarice of American industry. The nomads have short attention spans.

You can tell that the gypsies are going to have to move soon when the townspeople (who liked them for as long as they can make a buck trading with them) start to make fun of them.

Now let's talk (briefly) about the real issue behind sustainability in food and food production. It is popular to point to short-sighted activities in the private sector as examples of non-sustainability. And the stupidity of man certainly can produce such examples—whether clear-cutting, strip-mining, passenger pigeon shooting, bleaching and burning the soil with fertilizers, and so on. But in the world God made, all such dumb activities have a price tag. The real threat, the real danger, is that someone will develop an apparatus designed to keep those who incurred the cost from paying the price.

That apparatus is called the regulative state, and those who call for that apparatus to be expanded are those who are therefore the chief enemies of sustainability. In the long run we know (by definition) that that which cannot be sustained will not be sustained. But if we shuffle the costs off onto that poor mutt, the taxpayer, to the tune of katrillions, it will not be long before we won't know who did what, who owns what, or who pillaged what. The whole thing is unsustainable. Government with a thyroid condition is unsustainable. Every enviro, every foodist, every faddist, who therefore cries out to their savior (the one with the thyroid condition) to "do something" is a central, driving contributor to the myth that we can sustain an unsustainable lifestyle. If you want the best and most recent example of true unsustainability, take a look at our national budget.

Some may assume, by what I've written so far on creation and food and the whole ag-econ system that gets food on our plates, that I want to be nothing more than a shill for the status quo. However, this assumption would go clean contrary to quite a number of things I have written about it, including the paragraphs to follow.

Nothing written here should be taken as though I would be against any food production system that would result if all taxpayer subsidies were removed, and the regulative oversight of the nanny state were banished to the other side of Ganymede. I believe that a free people should be free to grow, harvest, sell, truck, shelve, freeze, process, buy, cook, or savor whatever they please, just so long as they do it on their own dime.

But in the meantime, the corporate food system is heavily regulated and subsidized by the state. The system is dislocated, and the dislocations all make their way down to us. Doing something about this would be great, but most of what is suggested or put forward is not really doing something. The economic system we are up against cannot be successfully attacked from this end *economically*.

The world's system can be attacked "from this end" by means of Word and sacrament, Christian community, prayer and psalms. They have no countermeasures for that. But they cannot be successfully dismantled by generating a fad that will just give Cargill something new to sell to us. It doesn't make sense to move from one end of the pool to the other because you are tired of being wet. Whether you buy at Walmart or Whole Foods, your money goes to a big corporation, and often the same one.

When the Church gets its act together, such that our influence moves into the economic stream in a transformative way, it will have an economic effect—which is quite different from having a political effect with economics as the means. Real transformation will result in a stream of money that stops going to the crony capitalists. But food fads just increase their opportunities, and their profits, by increasing the gullibility of the food-buying public. What does "fresh" mean? It means what the feds say it means. What does "organic" mean? It means what the feds say it means. What does "all-natural" mean? It means what the feds say it means, and this naturally results in absurdities.

And what happens when the search for sustainability sovereignty goes beyond the production of food to the production of eaters? One of my concerns about what (I think) underlies concerns about sustainability is that at the end of the day somebody is going to suggest that we should stop having kids. If I lived back in the day on my nice little sustainable farm, and had the same number of kids and grandkids that I have now, what would that mean? Say that we wanted to live as our agrarian ancestors had done, close to the land, laughter around a rough-hewn dinner table, and green beans to die for. That's all good, but say in the early days I was supporting myself and the fam on 100 acres. I have three kids and they each have five kids. Divvying everything up so that they can support themselves too means that by the time I am putting on my waders to cross over the Jordan, we have nineteen families with just over five acres each. In other words, the main pressure on sustainability is not caused by a nearby burgeoning city, but is rather caused by the attractiveness of a particular farm wife.

One of the striking things that I notice when reading histories and biographies is how the population scales have drastically changed. At the time of the Reformation, some of the most influential towns in Europe had populations that were just a fraction of population of the small town where I now live. When human populations grow (or explode), one of the things they do is forage. If you object to the costs of foraging, then the only thing you can do is call upon people to limit the number of children they have.

Related to this is the universal human tendency that people have to cluster in cities. Another universal human tendency has been to envy the lot of those who don't cluster there, those who get to live in the pristine countryside. But the game requires that you not to envy them so much that you might actually do something about it. Part of the romanticism about farmers is related to this—we respect them as part of their intangible pay, so that food continues to show up in the city, where we intend to live out our days.

We must never forget that the story arc provided in Scripture is an arc that begins with a Garden and ends with a Garden *City*. This allows for agrarian values (and I would argue requires them), but does not allow for agrarianism, if you follow the distinction. To want everyone to live close to the land is to want a human race that God, for some reason, decided not to create. But when the cumbersome size of the citified human race gets too much for certain "theories," that swollen human race is laid out on the Procrustean bed of the theory, and is sized to match. At one end of the bed is the ferocious agrarianism of Pol Pot and the Khmer Rouge; at the other end we have the more enticing blandishments of porn, pills and condoms. But the common thread is this—we could get ourselves a sweet little agrarian utopia going here, if it weren't for all these darn *people*.

But actual people matter more than theories do. When the gospel liberates a people, it sets them free to love one another more than they love their theories, and it also sets them free to get into problem solving. A free people are much more of a resource than they are a drain—because they solve problems *for* people instead of treating people as though they *were* the problem. "You, yes, you there, with your carbon footprint . . . you, you . . . breather!"

I have sometimes toyed with the idea of starting a local political party with three planks in the platform: 1. Release aquifer water so we can water our lawns *ad libitum*; 2. Eliminate the property tax; 3. Shoot the wolves. But whenever I make any comments about the aquifer, noting casually that the planet we live on is mostly water, the responders invariably point out to me, the slow one, that the oceans are salt water. But salt water is nothing but fresh water ore, and I bring this up to reinforce my point about people being a resource. I have absolutely no doubt that when the price of fresh water gets to a certain point (assuming a free market), some industrious lad is going to invent a cheap desalinator using materials that he found in his dad's shop in the garage, and he will go from being a smart boy to being a rich boy.

So here is the litmus test. If the theory depends for its success on all these irritating people shutting up, going away, or refusing to breed, then perhaps the theory is the thing that is not sustainable. P.J. O' Rourke summed up this problematic attitude aptly—"Too much of you, just the right amount of me."

CHAPTER 9

Food & Family

One manifestation of the stingy *no* of fatherlessness is in the way some wives pursue "healthy" menu choices for their home. By enacting stringent dietary regulations, they are inadvertently trying to teach their husbands and children *how to cheat*. In saying this, I do not wish to justify the sin of husbands who fail to stand up to their wives, or to justify a pattern of deception to work around the consequences of not standing up to them. I am saying that sin breeds more sin, and that each of us should repent of our own.

A school district in New York just recently dropped the First Lady's school lunch program because the kids were hungry all the time. What happens in a family where the first lady there has implemented a similar regime and does not have buy-in from her husband and kids? One of the obvious things is that the husband often has the resources to fix things at lunch with a greasy burger, after obtaining a vow from his co-workers to "not tell a soul."

A husband should not be given any encouragement (or apparent excuses) for living any kind of a double life. If that encouragement is foolishly given, he is still responsible for what he is saying and doing, but one of the purposes of marriage is to help us resist sin together—but too many husbands and wives live as stumbling blocks for one another. And a man should not work to put food on the table, his *own* table, and then come away from that table hungry.

One of the best scenes in the marvelous film *Sweet Land* is when Inge feeds Olaf a dinner with "just food." The sexual overtones are obvious, but are as wonderful as the dinner clearly was. And in both areas, it is crucial that the home not become a place of tight-fisted denial, where wives become the governess of *no*, instead of the mistress of *yes*. When that *no* happens, as a result the world outside is positioned to take up the role of promising satisfaction to cheaters. That is an invitation that many husbands need like a hole in the head.

So the cluster of motivations for our food confusions include father hunger, guilt, fear, acceptance of
manipulative doctrines, not to mention acceptance of
slanders against the goodness of God.

> Now the Spirit speaketh expressly, that in the lat-
> ter times some shall depart from the faith, giving
> heed to seducing spirits, and doctrines of devils;
> speaking lies in hypocrisy; having their conscienc-
> es seared with a hot iron; forbidding to marry,
> and commanding to abstain from meats, which
> God hath created to be received with thanksgiv-
> ing of them which believe and know the truth (1
> Tim. 4:1–3).

Food really is a big deal in Scripture, but oddly the
direction this importance takes is 180 degrees out
from what the hyperscrupulous want to require of us.
What is the bottom line in Scripture? Saying grace
with a full and sincere heart sanctifies the whole
smorgasbord, even if it is the kind you find under a
line of heat lamps in a cheap restaurant, and *even* if
there is enough MSG in the pans there to make your
spoon taste pretty good. Those who believe and know
the truth understand that God created food—including the weird stuff—to be received with *thanksgiving*.
What would a devil teach, given the opportunity? What doctrine might you expect to get from a

teacher whose conscience is sporting that tell-tale Lazy R brand? Well, the first thing a devil would want to teach is a prohibition of marriage. Too much sex involved. Second on his demonic killjoy list would be a whole host of banned foodstuffs, and given the state of the Church in the West today, it is not surprising that various food fads, allergies, diets, loathings and phobias are rampaging around in our midst. Because we live in fatherless times, no one appears to care enough for these poor people to say something simple, like "God is not *like* that." At the bottom of a lot of this is the inability to believe that God is a good *Father*. Fathers provide good things.

As I said previously, there *are* such afflictions as lactose intolerance. But you can't catch it from your friends, and if you find that more and more of your companions are fellow lactards, then something funny is happening. And that happening has more to do with picking up false doctrine from the *zeitgeist* than it has to do with some odd medical coincidence.

What may we receive with thanksgiving? Over what *kind* of meal may we bow our heads in true and reverent gratitude? Kraft macaroni in a box. Sirloin steak off the grill. Baked potatoes. Baked Alaska. Baked beans. Baked beans from a *can*. Clams and oysters. Blackened catfish. Marbled beef. Honeynut

Cheerios. Chocolate-Covered Sugar Blams. Green salad, Caesar salad, and art salad. Quarter-pounders. Strawberries. Whole milk. Goat cheese. Cabernet-Sauvignon. Kool-Aid. Green Jell-O. Food straight out of my garden. Food fresh from the factory. Skippy peanut butter. Apple jelly. Cinnamon toast. Wonder bread. Shredded wheat. Garbanzo beans. Gouda cheese. Velveeta. Roast duck. Rye bread. Krispy Kremes. Diet Pepsi. Creamed corn. Corn on the cob, picked fifteen minutes ago, and boiled five minutes ago. Almond chicken. An Arby's regular roast beef. Oatmeal stout. Real butter. Clotted cream. Bud Lite. Cream of wheat. Cold watermelon. Oreo cookies. Green beans. Green beans with pistachio nuts in them. Soy beans. Tofu. Yes, tofu. Swallow that reductio, *and* the tofu. Chicago-style hot dogs. St. Louis-style pizza. Movie theater popcorn. Enchiladas. Salt and vinegar potato chips. Cookie dough ice cream. Roast beast and gravy. Glazed ham. Cheese potatoes. And apple pie.

And why? Because God is our *Father*. In these our postmodern times, the relativists in the Church want to mix the Apostles' Creed up with about five gallons of paint thinner. But we must learn to take the Creed thick. "I believe in God the *Father* Almighty, Maker of heaven and earth." He made it, and arranged for it to come to your plate the way it has. So bow your head over it, full of gratitude, no matter what it is. And as you do, you are learning more and more . . . what God is like.

Body image issues also figure hugely in this cluster of motivations related to father hunger. When a girl who is hovering on the edge of "skeletal" sincerely believes in her heart that she is "fat," the problem is obviously one of a dominating paradigm of self-deception. And when this happens, such a person usually attracts the concerned attention of others, but only because (and this is my point) she took the problem too far. A lot of people have a milder version of the same problem, and no one is concerned at all.

Anyone familiar with the paintings of Rubens knows that different cultures have different notions about the feminine ideal. One time I was walking in a mall and a card shop had one of those lifesize cutouts of Marilyn Monroe outside the store, and I realized as I walked past that she was quite a little fireplug. A generation ago, the average Miss America was forty pounds heavier than today. And within certain limits, obviously that is just fine. There is no more reason for us to match the ideals of another generation than there is for them to match ours.

Unless . . . we move past questions of simple cultural taste. If, in the grip of screwed up notions of femininity, we start denying what God obviously wants to affirm, then we are in trouble. If an average girl starts to "eat healthy" and loses a bunch of weight (but does not go so far as skeletal), she will receive near universal praise and attention. And I have trouble believing that the affirmation she gets will be any less at church. She can look great to her husband, to her friends, and feel sexy and attractive, and all the rest of it. But if she drops below 13 percent body fat, and stops having her periods, and can't conceive a child, then it is clear that what she and all her friends call "eating healthy" is not healthy or natural or normal *at all*.

And this is because our culture has allowed its ideal of feminine beauty to be almost entirely detached from the teleology of the female body. And that can't be good. And this is why a number of healthy diets aren't at all. Healthy is as healthy does.

CHAPTER 10

A Pastoral Issue

F ather hunger issues are often mirrored in the church. When loving leadership is lacking in families, it's usually lacking in the church, as well. Too many pastors slip into the lazy, comfortable groove of paternal incompetence rather than guiding their flocks out of it by word and example.

I once read a tagline quip on the bottom of someone's email that was really quite profound—it said that if your pastor says that the wine in the Bible was really grape juice, then how can you believe *anything* he says?

Whenever someone stubbornly clings to foolish and thrice-disproven notions, it casts a shadow over everything else he says. Now I am not talking about the kind of mistakes we all make—I am talking about ideological commitments that are impervious to every form of evidence. This kind of thing contaminates everything else.

I say all this because the food fads that are circulating through the Christian world are so obviously bogus that it should cause us to question the soundness of everything else. Now of course I am not setting this up as my very own ideological litmus test. If someone teaches, simultaneously, that Jesus is Lord, and that a box of corn flakes shaken over your digestive tract will heal your constipation, the clear falsehood of the latter will not trump the former. But what it does mean is that you should not really be entrusting the care of your soul, and the souls of your family, *to someone who clearly does not know how to think*.

When it comes to our dietary habits and the rules of evidence, I have seen multiple examples of thought processes that were on the very same level with some shaman throwing chicken bones in the air to heal that pesky rash that you asked him to look at. And this from *Christians*. And there are pastors out there who teach this stuff, or encourage it, or go along with it, or fail to rebuke it.

These pastors either don't know any better, in which case they cannot be trusted to handle the sacred text of Scripture, or they do know better but are afraid of the coterie of health ladies in the church who are propagating this kind of nonsense, in which case their cowardice disqualifies them.

And that is my defense against those who say I've gone to meddlin' when it comes to food issues . . . that such a topic is outside my pastoral purview. Rather it is exactly where my attention belongs, because it is where the church's attention is being distracted from the truth. This topic has as clear a need as any for the application of Scripture and plain reason.

The church is capable of including any number of subcultural groups within her pale, and can do so without great difficulty. Ham radio operators, rodeo riders, surfers, and rock climbers are all welcome. And what they all do the Saturday before worship does not disrupt the reality of their worship together.

But food subcultures are a different matter. Food scruples are the deathly enemy of church unity. Every pastor is called by the Lord to hate food divisions, and every pastor who does not hate them is an enemy of his own peace. I don't want church splits, even if they come in a reusable bag.

The central pastoral issue of the New Testament was a dietary one—whether Jews and Gentiles could eat together. And if the apostle Paul fought so long and hard on this one—to keep the body of Christ from being divided this way—when the issue really was created by the laws of the Old Testament, how much more would he be militant about food divisions that resulted from an article that somebody read on the Internet?

I am not talking about genuine allergies. Everybody should know what those are. You serve your guest ground up peanuts in that Thai dish you've been wanting to try out, and forty five minutes later he looks like the Michelin tire boy, and the dinner party concludes late that evening in the ER. *That's* an allergy, and the apostle would not mind if we accommodated such food restrictions in charity. That is a beautiful opportunity to exercise charity—checking with those you invite about food restrictions.

But charity is called for on the other end also, and it has been abandoned by those who are afflicted with trendy allergies. Just as Paul tagged those unstable women who are always learning and never coming to a knowledge of the truth, so he would have identified the woman who became allergic to gluten because all her friends had recently become allergic to gluten, and she didn't want to be left out. This preserves the unity of *that* little group, but it plays havoc with the unity of the larger body. She and her friends are no fun to have over any more because she is always allergic to something, and it is always something new, and the last two times she was invited over, she brought her own food anyway.

This brazen rudeness is not called out for what it is because the people perpetrating it have a cover story created for them by the guy who is allergic to the Thai peanut thingy. You don't want *him* to die, do you?

Here is a rule of thumb. If you have ever showed up to a dinner party (not a potluck) unannounced with your own food, then you are an enemy of church unity. The Holy Spirit is working to unify the whole body in sweet table fellowship, and *you* are underfoot.

Here is another rule of thumb. If you are allergic to an ever-shifting list of the latest things to be allergic to, then you are actually allergic to charity. This is a bad condition to be in—if you are allergic to charity, then you are actually allergic to other people, church peace, and the Holy Spirit.

Last rule of thumb. If you think that every cook in the body has a bounden obligation to drop every other ingredient from her recipes if you are coming over, then perhaps you are waiting for the wrong person to make the sacrifice. Why don't you make the sacrifice, and just eat it? You might reply that this means that later in the evening you will have to deal with the icky angsty feelings that always accompany your consumption of your allergenic *du jour*. Well, isn't that a small price to pay because you love the brethren? Eat what is set before you—there's a strategy you could try (Luke 10:8). Better to *get* an imaginary rash on your body than to *be* a real rash on the body.

D.L. Moody once said that if you throw a rock into a pack of stray dogs, the one that yelps is the one that got hit. In a similar vein, the wicked flee when no man pursues (Prov. 28:1).

When I attack the trends that are conspiring to introduce food laws into the Church, and I point out that these food laws have a dubious ancestry, coming as they do from a wicked and perverse generation, do I mean to say that any Christians who don't eat exactly the way I do are wicked and perverse themselves? Of course not. There are Christians who eat way more leafy greens than I do who are much finer Christians than I am. Do I mean to introduce my own kind of inverse food laws into the Church, so that anyone who just wants to eat "just a little healthier" comes under suspicion? Of course not. What other people eat (if it has no higher authority than that they want to) is none of my concern or business. When other believers say grace over foods I think odd, I think it is wonderful. When they thank their Creator for their food, they are not talking to *me*.

Eating a little healthier is great, just so long as you are eating a little healthier than you were, and it is not cast to yourself as eating a little healthier than *he* is.

Do I think (or did I ever say?) that anyone who cares about stewardship of agricultural resources is a Marxist hippie who struggles with sexual perversion? No, actually. The cultural mandate back in Genesis requires careful stewardship of what God has entrusted to us—my central complaint about the stewardship shtick is that most of those urging it today are statists, and the state is the enemy of even the possibility of real stewardship. Stewardship is a basic Christian duty, which is why so many people want to pretend they are doing it. It is much easier to put a green decal on your car, or widen your phylacteries some other way, than it is to actually conserve something for real.

Anyone who doesn't see Tetzel all over again in the practice of selling carbon offsets (which you can now do at a stock exchange level), doesn't know the first thing about biblical worldview analysis. And if you don't know the first thing about how to see what a culture is actually doing, then you have no business teaching Christians what to do. If you don't understand the times, and you don't know what Israel should do, then you are not from the tribe of Issachar.

So, if I am not trying to do all these things, what am I doing? Who am I talking about? What's the point? The answer can be divided up into two categories. In the first place, I am critiquing one of the great spirits of the age, the teaching that is contained in books, articles and documentaries that is being insinuated into the Christian community. The false doctrine contained there can have really destructive effects in the lives of Christians, and as a pastoral counselor, I have more than once had a front row seat. Secular counselors have noticed some of the same pathologies—one doctor has even coined the phrase *orthorexia nervosa*— "an excessive focus on eating healthy foods."

The second category would be that of the Christian reader who wonders if I am talking about "*his* position." There is no telling from this distance, but if my qualifications are missed, if my point is inverted, if I am made to affirm what I have denied and vice versa, and if it is thought that I must hate farmers, then I probably am.

One of the larger pastoral problems in the church today is the trend to ever-increasing fruitiness, coupled with the cowardice of those who see what is happening, and yet say nothing.

Whenever someone proposes any particular pursuit in a singularly fruity way—and I am speaking of weird diets, oils with superpowers, medicinal odd-ballery, and other variations on the ancient spirit of haruspicy—and someone objects to it, one of the first things that will happen is that someone else will point out that there are all sorts of connections and remedies that we could not have anticipated beforehand. The whole world is weird. Well, yes, the world is weird, magical, uncanny, and penicillin is a fungus that kills bacterial diseases—*ho, ho, ho*. If we compare this to the folk remedy of trying to cure a sore throat by wrapping your neck in bacon before bedtime, which one is "weirder"? They are actually on the same plane.

But the point isn't weirdness at all. When I shake my head over the fruitiness of some proposed remedy, diet, or alignment of the furniture with cosmic forces, the point is never the odd juxtaposition of this with that. The world really is weird. But some things about it aren't weird at all. Let us invite Chesterton into our discussion, so that he may dispel our foolish superstitions with the laws that govern all magic. "If Jack is the son of a miller, a miller is the father of Jack. Cold reason decrees it from her awful throne: and we in fairyland submit."[7]

"There is an enormous difference by the test of fairyland; which is the test of the imagination. You

7   G.K. Chesterton, *Orthodoxy* (Chicago: Moody, 2009), 78.

cannot imagine two and one not making three. But you can easily imagine trees not growing fruit; you can imagine them growing golden candlesticks or tigers hanging on by the tail."[8].

So let us try to identify the locus of fruitiness. What is it exactly? I am not astonished at the prospect of a bacon wrap fixing a sore throat. The world is an odd place, and stranger things than that have been verified in double blind studies. I am astonished at the prospect of this being true because . . . because . . . because a superstitious somebody wants it to be, and because they wanted it to be true, they just decided it was.

Cold reason isn't weird, at least not in the way that the world is. Mundane epistemology is fairly pedestrian. How do you know it is raining? Well, I just came in from outside, and I am soaked. That which soaked me was falling out of the sky. Okay, I can buy that.

But if somebody else wants to tell me that it is raining in Tasmania right now because the bananas on their counter started to go brown a day earlier than they usually do, you will forgive me if my skepticism retains something of a robust character.

So the issue is practical epistemology, cross-checking, verification, and the authority of cold reason.

8 Ibid., 51.

The issue is not whether or not an astonishing and bizarre correlation might make it through that system of cross-checking. If something does make it through, as various magical things do, there will be no one more delighted than I.

This is not me standing on a pyramid constructed out of Enlightenment bricks. The Bible requires us to think this way.

> But refuse profane and old wives' fables, and exercise thyself *rather* unto godliness. (1 Tim. 4:7)

> . . . the older women likewise, that they be reverent in behavior, not slanderers, not given to much wine, teachers of good things— that they admonish the young women to love their husbands, to love their children, to be discreet, chaste, homemakers, good, obedient to their own husbands, that the word of God may not be blasphemed. (Tit. 2:3–5)

Certain tales tend to veer toward the frivolous and silly, and certain topics do not. Paul tells the godly older women to act like it, and to instruct the younger women on the great vocation of godly homemaking. Older women who do this are to be listened to. They are to be honored and heard. But there is another kind of old woman who is not to be listened to. Paul tells Timothy to "refuse" what they have to say. Turn away from it, have nothing to do with it. This kind of thing is destructive to the fellowship of the church. Pursue godliness instead. It doesn't say that we may pursue godliness by means of these silly, pointless fables. They are mortal enemies. One supplants the other. You can have godliness or you can have the juju beans migraine treatment, *but you can't have both*.

Note again. There is no conflict between godliness and a headache remedy that came from juju beans. If the next George Washington Carver makes something far better than peanut butter, both for jelly and for headaches, and he did it entirely out of juju beans, I will personally award him a Nobel Prize. There is no conflict between godliness and juju beans. *There is a profound conflict between godliness and credulity.*

Now, because some people who have a bent toward this kind of thing have trouble thinking with sufficient precision, it is not unlikely that I will be charged with attacking women, along with Paul. What's with using "old wives" as a pejorative? The reply is simple. As the contrast with the passage from Titus shows, the biblical position is that older women can have a fruitful ministry with the younger women. But if they decline to do so, there are certain sins that are characteristic of older women who are willing to talk about whatever comes into their heads. So one of those characteristic sins is the sin of silliness. The point is not that old wives are silly. The point is that silly old wives are silly.

There is one other point, and that is that *there is a pastoral duty* to warn and admonish the church against this kind of thing. Paul doesn't give us the content of the fables he had to deal with, but the word refers to a genus that has never lacked for content in any age.

One of the ways that pastors should shepherd their people in this regard is by encouraging husbands and fathers to pick up a sense of responsibility for what their wives are spending all their time talking about. Is it edifying? Or is it manifestly not? There are many husbands who need to man up. They need to learn how to do this because when these women are being silly, they are not being silly across the board. When it comes to managing cowardly husbands, they can be pretty shrewd.

CHAPTER 11

What Do They Teach Them in These Schools?

C.S. Lewis noted in his essay on the reading of old books that one of the great blessings of doing so is that it gets you out of your chronological provincialism. When you are stuck in your small town mentality, small differences are magnified and treated as though they were everything. But when you get out a bit more, you realize how much was held in common by everyone in that small town. The problem is that of the "invisible shared assumptions," which do not become visible until you get out into the wider world, and get a larger perspective. Old books, or books of history, help with this important task enormously.

This larger perspective is most necessary on the question of food and health, food and economy, and food and . . . food. Americans have been food faddists for a long time—centuries. And I am not speaking of splinter groups and odd communes. This is a mainstream phenomenon; it is what we do. Whenever the newest fad hits, we think it is really new because of the small differences between it and the previous fad, which previous fad had the misfortune of being successful enough to become the establishment. But if we walk up on the ridge outside this small town, we see how much this fad actually has in common with the one before it, and the one before that, and the one before that. It is our tradition to set up establishments, so that we can knock them down. And we invariably knock them down for the sake of the next establishment—diligently hiding from ourselves the manifest and plain realities of what we are doing. And the coming establishment will be every bit as temporary. How could it *not* be?

When someone asserts that it is "high time" that we as Christians learn to take "this issue" with the seriousness it deserves, we err if we rush to argue that particular point, pro or con. We must first take note of where we are. Who has the burden of proof? And do they have the burden of proof on their particular claim only, or do they also need to prove that they are doing something different than what a long chain of others with particular claims have been doing since the administration of Rutherford B. Hayes? I of course want to see evidence for whatever the particular claim is, but I would also love to see some kind of awareness of our long tradition of doing this same thing, over and over again. And in my experience that awareness is singularly lacking among zealous promoters. If it were not lacking, then by definition the food fad element disappears.

The American dinner table has been laden with absurd claims for a very long time. Suppose you had a young friend who had fallen in love, desperately, passionately, about seventeen times. When he came to you with news of the eighteenth lucky girl, and maintained stoutly that "this time it was different," would you not be dubious? And you would be dubious even though she actually could be different—but you would still be wise not take it on his say so.

Now suppose you had a friend who told you that you could determine whether or not you were allergic to peanut butter, or peanuts for that matter, by putting a dollop of peanut butter on the back of your right hand and extending it out parallel to the floor. And that if you could keep your arm straight then you were not allergic to the substances therein, and if you could not, then you were. What would you say?

Correct. You would say that such a person did not have a firm grasp on what constitutes the clear boundary between superstition and real knowledge. Further, you might conclude that you must have met this person in a fortune-telling shack outside Port-au-Prince, Haiti, at an establishment called Madame Santoni's.

But that is not necessarily the case—you may have met that person on the bus this morning, or he may work in the next cubicle at your high-tech engineering firm. He may exhibit a high level of intelligence, and be highly trained. But whether he is highly trained or not, he is certainly *not* highly educated. People who are highly educated don't believe that wet streets cause rain.

At the root here is a failure in the Church—we have not provided a fully-orbed Christian worldview, and we have not insisted that the leaders in the Church be *educated* men. We generally insist on a high level of training for ministry, but you can train a chimp to get the banana he wants by pushing on a lever. Ministerial "training," *bah*. Ministerial "training," *humbug*. We need men in the Church who know how to *think*, and not men who could in principle be snookered by the kind of spectral evidence once on display in Salem. "She *must* be a witch. I go *oww* every time she looks at me! See? Owwwww!"

As Chesterton once put it, if you don't stand for something, you'll fall for anything. But in order to stand for that something, you have to be *educated* in it. If you are merely trained to stand for something, then you have been indoctrinated, not educated, and you are not "standing" for anything really, except in the way.

I was recently interviewed on national radio by some good conservative people, and in the course of the interview there was a feast of reason and flow of soul. That was all good, but the thing that struck me upside the head was some of the *fruit*cake commercials in between the segments. You want to know why liberals are running the country? Because a bunch of ostensible conservatives think that fluoride (or fill this in with *your* icky substance of choice) causes whatever it is they want it to cause, rules of evidence be damned.

And no, if you put the dollop of peanut butter on the left hand, you haven't really addressed the problem. So how *do* we know things? How do we confirm things? With regard to any claim that matters enough that we need to check it, the Bible teaches that we look for external corroboration, internal consistency, and a clear willingness for the claim to be falsified.

"In the mouth of two or three witnesses shall every word be established" (2 Cor. 13:1).

"But neither so did their witness agree together" (Mark 14:59).

"He that is first in his own cause seemeth just; But his neighbour cometh and searcheth him" (Prov. 18:17).

Consequently, the big concern that I have about many believers going in big for foodie concerns, or those with treatments for designer allergies, or exotic treatments for various ailments, is not the proposed treatment itself. The issue is the nature of *knowledge*, not the nature of the stuff in the world. If oils made from pine needles were able to do marvelous things, there would be no one happier than I. But if no one is allowed to ask any judicious questions, then you may depend upon it—a scam is being run. We live in a world full of lies, and we are servants of the truth. Our approach should match that fundamental reality, and sadly, it often does not.

For any claim that is weighty, how can that claim be verified, and how can it be falsified?

So if I move to a different city, and am looking for a church, and I find out that the pastor of a church I am considering is big into some of this stuff (in the way that people are usually big into it), I wouldn't join that church. This is not because I care what he eats, or how he treats his joint pain. It would be because it is manifest to me that he does not know how the truth of an important matter is to be established. If, when it comes to his joint pain, he believes one witness, even though that witness contradicts himself, and he will not allow that witness to be cross-examined, then I know how it will go with *me* if a controversy ever arose. One incoherent witness testifying in the back room would be sufficient. "For we dare not make ourselves of the number, or compare ourselves with some that commend themselves: but they measuring themselves by themselves, and comparing themselves among themselves, are not wise" (2 Cor. 10:12).

And, by the way, it bears repeating here that whenever I strike at allergenic fads, I am *not* being harsh toward those with real allergies. To be critical of hypochondria is not the same thing as mocking the sick and infirm. Just the opposite, actually. The hypochondriac is the one who is mocking the sick.

In the latter part of the nineteenth century, a gentleman named Robert Koch came up with a method that has helped acquire much of our knowledge about illnesses. He developed a series of postulates to help identify the causal agents for various diseases. The basic outlines of this approach were that, first, the germ had to be found abundantly in every patient and in every diseased tissue; second, the germ must be isolated and grown in the lab; and third, the purified germ must cause the disease again in another host. So there you go, and makes good sense, doesn't it?

Koch had bacterial infections in the crosshairs, but since this is a matter of basic logic, the thinking supports questions about other issues, like viral infections and allergies.

So let me throw a couple other issues into the mix. I commented earlier on what I take to be the very foolish practice of determining allergies by means of muscular tests—if you can't hold your arm up when milk is dribbled on it, then you must be allergic to milk. But *educated* people do this, and the fact that Wilson thinks it is nuts doesn't even appear to be slowing them down.

Third item: A few years ago at the 2009 Auburn Avenue Pastors Conference, my friend Rich Bledsoe made the very important point that we have discovered that the world is a very complicated place, and that causation is frequently a matter of how things function in a complex web. Causation is not necessarily like a single file of thirteen cars having themselves a pile-up on the interstate. It is very rarely completely isolated, as it is when you put the eight ball in the corner pocket. A number of scientific developments have alerted us to this truth, largely by rubbing our noses in it—causation is not simple.

Now before we learned this, conventional approaches to things like medicine, or nutrition, or determining allergies, had a clear tendency toward reductionism. Koch's postulates above make wonderful sense to me, but if you apply them a truncated form, and treat the patient in front of you as though he were simply a car needing a bit of work on the carburetor, then you will eventually provoke a reaction. As medical science advanced, we discovered we were (as often as not) dealing with complex *systems*, and not with just one thing in isolation. And in that environment, if a group of practitioners arise, claiming that they want to treat the "whole person," they will be greeted with relief by many.

So I happen to believe that many of the criticisms leveled against conventional approaches to medicine, nutrition, allergies, and so forth, were quite fair so far as they went. The world *is* more complicated than that, and the human body is fearfully and wonderfully made. I am quite prepared to admit, and *gladly*, that the world is an odd place, and that we might discover odd treatments for odd ailments in odd places. I am singularly broadminded on the topic. It may well be that the cure to cancer is lurking, even today, in an average bowl of corn flakes. That would be okay by me.

So then, why do I find it funny when people determine allergies by the dribbling milk method? The central point to make is that it is *not* because the *treatment* is odd or funny. If you think about it, every treatment for every ailment is odd or funny. The whole world is odd and funny.

But if this is being done because we have now discovered complex "systems," and the vast web of causation, and integrated approaches to the whole person, then shouldn't the standards for being able to decipher it all go *up*, not down?

When systems get complicated enough, one of two things can happen. The first is that we winnow out the number of experts, and we get ourselves some real experts around here. Before, back in the simple causation days, we had five thousand experts. Now that we understand the enormous complexity of these systems, we have fifty experts and practitioners. But what are we to make of it all when an acknowledgement of the complexity of the systems turns everybody and his cousin into an expert and internet-trained practitioner? We used to have five thousand experts—now we have five hundred thousand.

This is the second thing that can happen when a sense of the complexity of the systems settles in—we now understand how complex everything is, *so that now anybody can pretty much say anything he wants.* Nobody appears to understand anything really, and so you can set up shop without fear of contradiction.

Returning to the top, Koch's postulates *could* be applied in a mechanical and reductionistic way, but at the end of the say, they still make good solid horse sense. They make good sense because they are a matter of common sense and applied logic. They aren't the end of the story, because systems are often more complex than one thing doing another thing, and you found both of them in ten minutes, look at you go. Isolating the butler's fingerprints on the gun doesn't give you the whole complex story, but it does give you a significant part of it.

In a similar way, here is my postulate. If there is an inverse relationship between the complexity of the universe and the education, training, and intelligence of its purported interpreter, then what you have is just one step up from shamanism, if that. My postulate, incidentally, leaves plenty of room for the independent genius, for the complex systems analyst, and the unconventional researcher. God bless all those guys.

What it doesn't leave room for is a group of teenagers on a lark discovering one another's milk allergies in the kitchen. Why don't I believe those teenagers? Because the world is a complex place, and the body is fearfully and wonderfully made. There are many factors that could be involved in their reactions, and I don't believe that as the complexity of systems goes up, the qualifications to interpret them goes down. I don't believe that wisdom in the world can be achieved by means of diluted homeopathic training.

CHAPTER 12

The Table of Gratitude and Love

The world is full of friendly rivalries, and when they get unfriendly in any serious way, most people observing can see it for what it is—a personal problem. Fords and Chevrolets, PCs and Macs, microbrews and macrobrews, and so on. There are other preference choices that *ought* to be in this category, but for some reason they are not. Do you want your corn fresh or store bought? Or, more accurately, do you prefer having corn that is store bought, as opposed to not having superior fresh corn? Ya pays yer money and ya takes yer choice. Nobody (and by this I mean nobody here) has any complaint whatever against Christians who use their Christian liberty to seek out food they like, and who eat it with gratitude and zest. It doesn't matter if it involves sushi, tofu, or Skippy peanut butter. Thanksgiving *sanctifies* all foods, and go, team.

So in what follows, if the food issues discussed *are* in this *adiaphora* category for you, covered over with multiple layers of gratitude, well, then, good for you and I am not talking about you. But if the sentiments are religious or quasi-religious (as they frequently are these days), then I *am* talking about you. Foodism in America constitutes a *significant* false religion, and there are way too many Christians who do not realize the extent of their syncretistic compromises. There are multiple issues involved, and they are all connected. As Luke, my son-in-law puts it, these are not individual mushrooms. Get sufficient distance and you can see the whole fairy ring.

There are three basic points to make here. First, foundationally, Christians have been drifting into an adoption of a sentimentalist hermeneutic instead of a rational and logical hermeneutic. God gave us minds so that we could study and understand. But even in conservative Christian circles, there is a rising suspicion of intellect that is quite alarming. Secondly, Christians have been giving way to a spirit of murmuring and ingratitude, even though

God gave us hearts so that we could be grateful. And last, because we have inverted head and heart, we have found ourselves saddled with a guilt-ridden, works-righteousness approach to our daily bread. How many Christians torture themselves with self-rebuke because they aren't "eating healthy enough?" They didn't have a whole lot of time for lunch yesterday, so they didn't walk the three blocks necessary to get that bean sprout sandwich, and instead just stopped at the street vendor on the first corner. Instead of feeling guilty, though, they ought simply to have *thanked God for the hot dog*. What? Too spiritual to thank God for a hot dog? We have the problem summed up right there.

I said we have inverted head and heart. God gave us minds to *think* with and hearts to *thank* with. Instead we use our hearts to think about the world as we would like it to have been, and we use our minds to come up with rationalizations for our ingratitude. We are a murmuring, discontented, unhappy, ungrateful people. And because we think we want salvation from our discontents, we cook up one cockeyed thing after another. God will be pleased if we eat raw foods, or unprocessed foods, or brownish foods, or unsprayed foods. God will also be pleased if we eat organic apples that were sprayed with that all natural coyote urine instead of being sprayed with that un-natural tetragylcyramadamboni.

We think we are well-advanced in worldview thinking, as we like to call this nonsense, when we actually haven't gotten past "God is great, God is good, let us thank Him for our food."

We can look to the Lord's Table to learn this gratitude.

The most important things about food are the companions, seated around the table. The second most important thing is the table itself, the fact of the gathering. The third most important thing would be the quality of the food consumed. We learn all of this from the First Table, the Lord's Table, and we are called to imitate it in the rest of our lives. Food disorders—among which I include false doctrines about food—arise from getting these priorities out of order.

I have written at length about the Lord's Table in many other places, and so will not undertake to show here what I have tried to demonstrate there—suffice it to say that all our eating, with necessary adjustments made, should be following after the general pattern of eating established for us in the Table. But while I don't want to establish all this again here, I do need to assert it again—before we sing the song concerning family meals, we need to get the pitch.

The Lord's Table should be regular, observed whenever God's people assemble together as summoned. We are the family of God, and part of this is demonstrated in the fact that we eat together. As I understand the Scriptures, this means weekly communion. Second, the Lord's Table is a feast, not a fast, and is a time for rejoicing and celebration, not a time for afflicting our souls. It is eucharist, thanksgiving. Third, it should be observed with wine that has alcohol in it and bread that has gluten in it. No Christians should avoid those elements on the authority of their own choices or preferences.

There are many things that can be gleaned from this, but here are three to work with now. First, eating should be a social event. Eating alone should be an anomaly. When we eat, we should seek out companions. The word *companion* comes from the Latin and refers to someone with whom we break bread together. Second, eating should be a joy and a comfort, not a soulless refueling. Even in times of grief, as after a funeral, eating together is not a wail of misery but a reassurance and a comfort. And apart from such particular times of grief, meals should be times of laughter, stories, communion, sharing, giving, and more laughter. And third, God gave us a meal that contains elements that really *get* to gnostics. Grape juice and flat crackers for communion are a fitting description of the gospel we are presenting to the world.

Christians who are concerned that their food life be healthy—and that should include all of us—should therefore concentrate on these three things. Whatever we do, Paul says, we should eat and drink to the glory of God. Eat together on a daily basis with people who love you, and whom you love. Second, make it a ritual appointment. Sanctify a place, a dining room table, say, and show up there at the appointed times. Now I can guarantee you that if these two things are in order, the food that will appear on that table, *whatever it is*, will be worth saying grace over. The gratitude will not be misspent.

"Better [is] a dinner of herbs where love is, than a stalled ox and hatred therewith" (Prov. 15:17). We have two variables here, which means we have four possibilities. We can get from this passage the main point, and then, for our purposes, a secondary point. The main point is that our two mentioned options are a scarce meal with love and an abundant meal with hatred. The two not mentioned are a scarce meal with hatred and an abundant meal with love. The proverb sets our priorities for us. If we love one another, we can overlook the fact that we are having to eat like vegans. And if we hate each other, there is not a French chef in the world who can make a sauce that will cover up that acrid taste. Having set our priorities this way, we see that love is the crucial thing to have at the table, and that hatred is the enemy to be forever banished. Now the proverb also presupposed a sliding scale on the matter of lesser importance, on the question of what we eat—a meal of herbs on the down side to the meat of a stalled ox on the swank side. We should rather have the most important thing, love, even if it means taking the downgrade meal on the scale of less important things.

We have been blessed with great abundance, and we should rejoice in that abundance. We should be generous and ready to share, but we should not feel guilty about the abundance that God has given. To feel guilty is actually to *be* guilty of another sin, that of ingratitude. This means that we have the privilege of grilling the meat from the stalled ox, *and* sitting down with people we love.

The other option not mentioned is instructive as well. Food cranks are judgmental, harsh, unforgiving, strident, and severe. If you invite them over they feel free to sit in judgment (vocally) on whatever is being served, and on the content of *all* your cupboards for that matter. They show up for dinner at your house with their own food, not because they are being generous with it, but because whatever you were going to serve them has cooties in it. In short, you find yourself eating a meal of herbs alongside someone who has a hypercritical eye. The vocalized criticism of the menu is not thought by them to be rudeness because they have assumed a spiritual position. They have taken a *moral* stand, and hence every conceivable rudeness is therefore justified. You have found yourself, my friend, in the worst of both worlds.

In summary, in descending order of preference:

1. Filet mignon and a table of joy. Sing for gladness.

2. Turnip greens and a table of joy. Sing for gladness.

3. Filet mignon and hateful piercing stares. Ick.

4. Turnip greens and fierce denunciations of any who stray from the turnip green way, even in their hearts for a moment. Get me *out* of here.

I mentioned earlier that there was a secondary point to be made, and here it is. The stalled ox is mentioned as a luxury item, which it was, but there is no hint of disapproval for the practice of confining an ox to the stall. If it were a sin to eat such meat that was raised with tenderness-on-the-plate in view, then this would be an odd illustration. We see the same thing in the parable of the prodigal son in Luke 15—what does the father famously order the servants to butcher? The *fatted* calf, and not a calf who was unfortunately and quite accidentally on the portly side. One lexicon defines the word *fatted* from Luke as meaning to "feed with wheat, to fatten." As we work through this, we have to be careful not to let sentimentalism dictate our standards to us.

The faithful Christian looks around the table, sees who is sitting with him, and he loves them. The fellowship and thanksgiving sanctify whatever is on the table—and pretty much anything can be on the table. If we can get it down, there is not much that gratitude can't sanctify (1 Tim. 4:4).

The mentality of unbelief approaches the problem in quite a different fashion. This mentality wants to focus on the nature of the food, and provided *that* is copacetic, then the people around the table are thereby approved.

Which sanctifies which? The gold the altar or the altar the gold? Having established the principle, *i.e.* that the altar does the sanctifying, we have to ask, in matters of table fellowship, whether the altar is on the platters or in the chairs.

The criteria for approved food can cover a vast range. There are denominational differences within this broad outlook—there are factions that support "like mom used to make," high end restaurant food, food eaten by manners snobs, food applauded by organic foodies, social justice food, my ethnic food as over against your ethnic food, food that doesn't provoke my phantom allergies, food that has not been contaminated by microwave cooties, and more. You name it, we can supply the necessary food coloring that will help us divide the body of Christ. We draw divisions on the table, and the necessary result is divisions between those in the chairs. But Jesus hates the latter a whole lot worse than He *might* hate the former.

So here is your test—and this is one of the first lessons the New Testament church was required to master, long before Nicea or Chalcedon. When the Gentiles showed up in the church, some of them continued to eat their bacon. What is more important to you? The presence or absence of bacon, or the presence or absence of Demetrius?

Imagine you have been invited to dinner somewhere, and suppose you just can't get past the fact that your hosts are, apparently without malice, serving up carcinogens covered in gravy. Well, Jesus said that we had to take up our cross in order to follow Him. Your obligation is to die for your brother. At least in this case your obligation is covered in hot gravy.

Uptight food scruples, as they commonly operate in the church today, are an insult to justification by faith alone, the principal glory of which is table fellowship (Gal. 2:14–16). Pastors should be far more jealous on the point than they are. But confronting food divisions within a congregation takes courage, and we think the apostle Paul used all of that kind of courage up.

The basic food law for Christians is love. The basic food law for Christians is that of reducing friction to table fellowship. Adding diet barriers increases potential points of friction. Whenever diet barriers are necessary for medical reasons (as they sometimes are), we should work with them, *of course*. But we should all recognize what our shared goal should be—free table fellowship, for all Christians, in every direction. Two Christians, with completely different brown bag lunches, should be able to laugh and talk together over those lunches, even though one bag is filled with food that is full of pure thoughts and the healthiest thing to do with the other lunch would be to eat the bag itself.

Whenever I write about food, which I am constrained pastorally to do, one of the standard dismissive responses that I see in comments on my blog and web chatter is that I am not educated on the subject, that I have not read the right studies, etc. But I am not making these observations as a *food* expert (though I am reasonably well-read on the subject). I am making these observations as someone who has been studying

people in depth for four decades or so. I couldn't recognize gluten under a microscope to save my soul, but
I can recognize monkey-see-monkey-do when I see it.
I do know how to identify a young woman with dad-
dy issues that are all heaped up on her nearly empty
plate. I know what food wowserism looks like. I can
recognize a green produce pecksniffian. I know what
a moralistic crusade looks like.

For those whose food choices are different from
mine, and who are *not* doing these weird people
things, then I am quite prepared to bless God for every
one of their menu choices. Honestly. But to appeal to
that great Seinfeld line—"People! They're the worst!"

So the issue is the *people*, never the food. Jesus declared all food, as such, clean. He didn't just declare
what I like clean. He declared the following clean—
sun-dried raisins, bacon, clam chowder, tofu, GMOs,
Wonder bread, Grape-Nuts, and the yogurt, strawberries and granola I just had for breakfast. When
the food is just food, and God is thanked for it, and
there are no hidden ideological agendas, I couldn't
care less what my brother eats and neither could
God. I wouldn't dream of taking him to a restaurant
and ordering for him. And when he orders, I wouldn't
dream of turning up my nose at his choice, saying,
"You know, studies have shown . . ." Okay, I might say

something if he ordered grits with shrimp, but only in a jolly, comradely way.

As one sage has said, knowledge is knowing that a tomato is a fruit. Wisdom is not putting it in the fruit salad. This principle of knowledge and wisdom applies to more than just tomatoes.

What is the balance to be kept when it comes to saying that God "doesn't care what you eat," which He doesn't, and saying that we are to exercise dominion in all that we do? If there is no neutrality anywhere, and there isn't, then how does this fit with statements like "God doesn't care"?

The answer is that God's cares about everything, but He doesn't care about them the same way we do. Our job is to learn how to care the *way* He does, instead of invoking His name to make it seem like He cares the same way we do. There is a way that seems right to a man, but the dead end of that cul–de–sac is death (Prov. 14:12). Men have a way of esteeming things that God considers below dumpster scrapings. "And he said unto them, Ye are they which justify yourselves before men; but God knoweth your hearts: for that which is highly esteemed among men is abomination in the sight of God" (Luke 16:15).

So there no neutrality anywhere, but this is not the same thing as saying that everything matters in the way we want it to. For example, say that somebody started saying that a particular brand of white T-shirt was guaranteed to make you holier, wiser, and healthier than you are now. I would be willing to say that God doesn't care about whether you wear that T-shirt or not because His Word leaves that kind of decision up to us and our preferences. But this doesn't make us "T-shirt neutral." God cares if those who made it were doing the best job they could given their resources, He cares if we cheat people or not when we sell it, He cares if it was shoplifted, He cares whether it is folded in a drawer or dumped on the bed all the time, and He cares if we make spurious claims about how holy, wise, and healthy it might make us. If someone claims that this tee-shirt he is selling can cure my cancer, and I dispute it, it is not an adequate comeback for him to say, "I thought you believed there is no neutrality!" There isn't, but "no neutrality" doesn't anything can do everything.

So bring it down to food. It is not remembered often enough that the Pharisees were pushing, in part, a pure foods movement. But the problem was not with their food—it was the leaven that they insisted on putting into everything. Jesus warned us about that leaven, and not about the food *per se*. Jesus had no problem going to a Pharisee's house for a Pharisee dinner, and when you do that you are going to get Pharisee food (Luke 7:44). But Jesus was strict in his warning to His disciples—watch out for the leaven of the Pharisees (Matt. 16:11–12). Beware of their *teaching* concerning food, not the food as such.

We know from Scripture what food tastes like without that leaven. The Bible tells us plainly. "For the kingdom of God is not meat and drink; but righteousness, and peace, and joy in the Holy Ghost" (Rom. 14:17). "For every creature of God is good, and nothing to be refused, if it be received with thanksgiving: For it is sanctified by the word of God and prayer" (1 Tim. 4:4–5). The world is God's bistro, and the menu is enormous. The bottles in the middle of every table at God's bistro are full of righteousness, peace, joy, and thanksgiving. It is a special sauce, and it goes on anything.

So why do I say that God doesn't care what you eat? Well, because, you know, because of the verses that say the same thing. And why do I also say that the glory of God is involved down to the last caramelized onion? Because the Bible says that whatever you eat, it should be to the glory of God (1 Cor. 10:31). But this concerns the *way* we come to food, not what food we come to. Jesus declared all foods clean (Mark 7:19). When He declared all foods clean, He was not declaring all food-fussery clean. Just the opposite. Declaring all foods clean means that every attempt to make the foods unclean again is a vain form of uncleanness. It won't work—the food cannot be defiled by this teaching, but the hearts *can* be.

So—righteousness, peace, joy, and thanksgiving, all of them in green bottles. By way of contrast, the foodie movement as it exists in its natural state, *at its point of origin out in the world*, consists of fear, anxiety, self-righteousness, timidity, guilt, ingratitude, and pride. It is a warehouse of fifty gallon drums full of Pharisaical leaven. Anybody who cannot see that reality is simply not paying attention. So when Christians go over there to get some food, I don't care—because God doesn't care what's in your *food*. He cares what is in your *heart*. So I don't care if you get your food at Safeway or at the Coop. You have to buy it somewhere. Just make sure you get some, and make sure you thank God for it.

God doesn't care what is in your food, but He cares very much what is in your food-thoughts. So what a pastor must care about is whether Christians are picking up any of the *leaven*—the fear, anxiety, self-righteousness, and so forth. And the answer is that they are, and in many cases, in terrible, debilitating ways. One of the ways I know this is the case is the inability of some to grasp these very simple distinctions. All foods are clean. Not all hearts are. Everything else follows.

I am afraid I can't really finish making this point as I would like to without bragging a bit about Nancy again, but (truth be told) I don't mind doing that. Anybody who has read my thoughts on food might easily gather that I take a dim view of food righteousness. That would be right. And they may have read me saying that "God doesn't care what you eat." But does this mean that God doesn't care *how* we eat, or *why* we eat? Or with whom? Of course not. The world is God's bistro, remember, and the production and consumption of food is necessarily a big part of all our schedules.

So food is a big deal at our house, not a little deal. Every Saturday night we have our Sabbath dinner, where Nancy spends her Saturdays preparing a thanksgiving meal for thirty-five people, and that is if there is no company—and there is frequently company. *And* she uses cloth napkins. One time she was ironing the cloth napkins, which are not just for Sabbath dinner, incidentally, and I asked why she was doing that. She said, putting it all in a nutshell, "It's reformational."

So meals are about loving people with something hot for the plate. Meals are about loving people with pressed cloth napkins. Meals are about joy and laughter across the table. Meals are about the pandemonium of clean-up. Meals are a big deal. We should love them more than we do, and this means receiving God's permission slip to eat absolutely anything, and then with equal joy and grace to receive His commandment to love the person sitting across from you.

Made in the USA
Columbia, SC
04 December 2018